To Pamela,

The love of my life, and more than I ever deserved.

DEDICATION

This book, published posthumously on behalf of our father, Terry De La Porte, is dedicated to The Leader who dwells inside each of us. The lessons imparted through him hold the potential to awaken your inner Leader, and our hope is that Dad's wisdom will enrich your life and the lives of all those who follow you.

—Jason De La Porte, Dawn Leath and Kim Haight

TABLE OF CONTENTS

FOREWORD

Terry De La Porte was a man who lived 57 full years. He was a man whom God blessed with many talents and rewarded in every area of his life.

On the outside, Terry had it all—the perfect marriage with his childhood sweetheart, Pam, for over thirty-eight years and a beautiful family and grandkids that adored him and looked to him for guidance, strength, and wisdom. Yet those who had the pleasure of truly knowing Terry understood that what made him so special was Whom he had working with him on the inside.

He was wealthy and accomplished much. He worked with managers, directors, and high-level executives in over thirty industries. His clients became friends because of Terry's desire to genuinely understand their challenges, help solve their problems, and achieve things that—in many cases—had never been done before.

His talents also spilled into sports. Terry was an avid golfer and college basketball star. He spent much of his life multiplying these talents with hundreds of kids who had the honor of playing for him as he coached basketball and baseball.

Terry was a man with noteworthy ethical standards, daunting goals, and big dreams. One of his remaining dreams was the publishing of this book.

When Terry was diagnosed with pancreatic cancer in early May 2004, it looked like this final dream might not be realized, for there was no plan in place. Then Tate Publishing entered our world, and in accordance with God's perfect plan and timing, Terry's great dream became a reality.

A special thanks must go to Kim House—not only for bringing Tate Publishing to the table, but for working so diligently to organize the book you are about to read and leading it into production.

Terry spoke constantly about leaders and leadership. His belief was that the ultimate measure of leadership is legacy. And so it is this book, among many other treasures, that it will allow the legacy of Terry De La Porte to live on for years to come in the hearts and minds of those who remain and those who learn from his wisdom.

THE ANTECEDENT, CONTEXT, AND CHALLENGE

October 5, 2003

It was June of 1980, and I had recently announced my resignation as Vice-President of Personnel & Training for one of McDonald's Corporation's largest and most successful franchises.

I had felt a calling to pursue a purpose. The purpose was to develop other leaders, managers, employees, and organizations by opening a Southwest-based training and consulting business.

My planning turned very quickly to the process of, *What does a Christian businessman need to focus on to ensure that the formation of his business fulfills God's plan and design for an organization?*

I searched bookstore after bookstore, counseled with other Christian business people, and sought out various pastors. Very little information was located, and no books addressed this leadership dilemma to my satisfaction. It was at this time that I decided answers did exist, and the pursuit of those questions began. More by default than plan, I decided to look at the Bible as a "management book" with God as its author.

Through the inspired teaching and preaching of three pastors, Reverend Norm Boshoff, Reverend Gerald Farley, and Dr. Charles Lowery, the Scriptural connections were revealed. After over twenty-five years in the training and education field, the concepts and skills are becoming increasingly clear as to what is in alignment with "Christ's Model" and what is outside his plan.

However, many ideas and concepts sound good. Many are even supported by well-known scholars, educators, business leaders, politicians, consultants, authors, major universities, and corporations. This endorsement does not guarantee the validity of the concept, idea, or skill. We must learn to discern and evaluate from a new paradigm. I believe this new context is Christ as a Leader.

So how is the average, well-meaning, and motivated person to know if this idea, principle, book, concept, or theory is valid? How will we know it is the one we should adopt in order to become a great leader?

The answer is really quite simple. We measure the information offered against the example set by **The Perfect Leader, Jesus Christ.** If we can study and learn from Reagan, Kennedy, Thatcher, Covey, Peters, King, Gandhi, and countless other enlightened, talented leaders and scholars, then why not learn from the greatest?

As a Christian who views Christ as my personal Savior and the only man to walk this world without fault, it is an easy jump for me to see his leadership as perfect. I believe his example is appropriate to model. After all, millions are still pursuing his vision. His organization has grown for over 2000 years. His followers continue the quest with fervor. He has given us the Bible to study, learn, act upon, and to validate his leadership.

For those who are reading this book and do not believe Christ to be their personal Savior, the content of these chapters should be no less compelling. It is hard to deny the impact this man has had on the world or its people. For nearly 2000 years the example moves forward, to every country and corner of the world. His leadership has provided hope, direction, and unparalleled ethical standards. His leadership has been the driving force behind the formation and defense of nations. It has had major impacts on economies, culture, and religion. **All of this was accomplished in just three short years of ministry here on earth.** That is leadership! Even to the skeptics, it builds a strong case that this could very well be — The Perfect Leader.

His leadership influence has witnessed and endured persecution, praise, prosperity, and pestilence, but it always survives and grows.

It is this leader — Jesus Christ, all-knowing God — that modeled the example. It is my purpose to connect Christ's model with today's trends, theories, and strategies. If I can validate that Christ used a particular approach or skill, then I believe it serves not only as a model for us to follow but a challenge to lead in this manner. We could then answer the question as to how we should build our businesses, organizations, and grow our people.

On the other hand, if Christ's Model contradicts a philosophy or theory, I believe the opposing theory to be a false approach, unworthy of our attention or adherence. The intent of the following chapters is not to focus on what we should avoid, but the characteristics and approaches we should implement.

I am not a theologian or even an expert on the Scripture. I am a businessman — intent on developing an organization based on solid leadership fundamentals. These fundamentals should guide me in creating the type of environment that will provide motivation to excel within the hearts of our employees.

The task at hand seems overwhelming. I have asked myself numerous times, *Am I the right person to undertake this project?* I have collected notes on this topic for over ten years, and the thought of organizing these thoughts into a book has gained in both urgency and focus. I claim four Scriptures as my verification that this book is on purpose. Unless noted, all Scripture will be quoted from the New International Version, NIV.

> Exodus 4:12 "Now go; I will help you speak and will teach you what to say."
>
> Jeremiah 29:11 "For I know the plans I have for you," declares the Lord, "plans to prosper you

and not to harm you, plans to give you hope and a future."

Romans 15:4 "For everything that was written in the past was written to teach us, so that through endurance and the encouragement of the Scriptures we might have hope."

II Timothy 3:16–17 "All Scripture is God-breathed and is useful for teaching, rebuking, correcting and training in righteousness, so that the man of God may be thoroughly equipped for every good work."

Leadership is a responsibility that must be taken seriously. It is through leadership that the future is shaped. It is through leadership that our businesses fulfill their purposes while acting out our ethics, priorities, and beliefs. It is through leadership that our personal lives are allowed to influence the lives of our followers, friends, clients, and family.

The Perfect Leader is very clear on the goal. II Corinthians 13:11 gives us a challenge that will require our best and that will continuously drive us to improve.

" . . . Aim for perfection, listen to my appeal, be of one mind, live in peace."

The target is clear; we listen only when there is something worthwhile to hear. There must be "one" best way, and our outcomes will have better results with fewer hassles and less stress. This is a liberal, but rewarding, way to look at this message.

The challenge is not to be perfect, but to aim for perfection—to be all that our talents and intellect will allow us to be. To aim for perfection, we must have a model of perfection. The model of perfect leadership is Christ. (Chapter 1 will go into depth on this characteristic of a leader.)

Leadership is as much an attitude as it is a behavior. I can find no Scripture that tells us our behavior must be like Christ.

He knew our actions would fall short; therefore, He discourages our pursuit of perfection. Philippians 2:5 tells us, "Your attitude should be the same as Christ." Evidently, our intentions and motives weigh more than our delivery. However, those who can never seem to get their actions and intentions to align are soon seen to be untrustworthy and lacking credibility. Good intentions without appropriate delivery will result in mistrust and failure. To guarantee our actions, the modeling of our intentions after Christ, additional awareness, knowledge, and skills are required. Then we can expect to deliver our intent with aligned action.

It is this attitude that will help us seek out wisdom, skills, and counsel to improve our behavior. Intent is critical to leadership. Intent is also critical to following and pursuing the model of The Perfect Leader.

The intent of this book is to challenge each reader to become a better leader than you were before approaching these pages. We must be able to fulfill the command given to us in Romans 12:2.

> "Do not conform any longer to the pattern of this world, but be transformed by the renewing of your mind. Then you will be able to test and approve what God's will is—his good, pleasing and perfect will."

We must learn to discern the approaches to leadership. Through my experience as an executive, coach, mentor, consultant, and trainer for many of our nation's largest and smallest businesses, I have been exposed to many trends, theories, philosophies, and practices. While many are on solid ground, there are numerous methodologies that are based on humanism, manipulation, fear, or control. They are miles away from the model of The Perfect Leader.

The Scriptures will provide evidence that The Perfect Leader modeled vision, was always on purpose, used teams, empowered his followers, and set clear consequences while being a great communicator. In the following chapters, many of these characteristics as well as others will be explored. These attributes will then give us a backdrop for examining today's leadership challenges.

My prayer is that your leadership focus will become clearer as you develop a training plan to create alignment between your leadership and that of The Perfect Leader. Through this alignment, you will become a "living letter" and an example of a great leader. I believe this to be possible by learning the lessons from above, which are modeled and recorded by The Perfect Leader.

While growth and change are not easy, they are requirements and necessities in a dynamic life. With the guidance and encouragement provided within this book and the inspiration and wisdom of The Perfect Leader the journey will lead to change and fulfillment—a new plateau in our leadership and influence.

CHAPTER ONE

PERFECT LEADER QUALITY #1:

AIM FOR PERFECT

BUT AVOID BEING A PERFECTIONIST

*"Aim for perfection, listen to my appeal,
be of one mind, live in peace."*

II Corinthians 13:11b

AIM FOR PERFECTION

The first thought that came to my mind when I saw this challenge was why "aim" and not "be"? The action word given us is an interesting image. Aim implies a conscious effort on my part—one that has both a target in mind and requires full attention and focus. More importantly, when put in the context of the target of perfection, it obviously indicates a lifelong journey.

What an awesome challenge for a leader to undertake. A challenge to stay focused for a short time is taxing; to aim for perfection as a lifelong journey—that is a commitment that is life changing. Thank goodness, the action is *aim* and not *be*.

What does aim for perfection mean to the twenty-first-century businessperson? The key is not a single step, but a series of steps beginning with knowing the target. Later chapters will deal with the targets (vision and mission). The strategy includes a process of creating, planning, executing, adjusting, and refining.

The strategy will also translate to stability with our eyes

"aimed" at the target. It is our consistency of focus that provides the island to our followers during the frequent storms of change.

According to The Perfect Leader, there are two critical issues facing us as leaders at this time. They are the ability to exercise wisdom (experiences witnessed as skills) and understanding (applied knowledge leading to informed choices).

Before you take issue with my definitions, take a look at the original use of language. The reference below describes the building of a house and the communication within its walls to create a lasting domain. The Greek word used to describe wisdom is *chormah,* the root word for our word skills. Understanding translates to *tetunah,* our word for choices.

> Proverbs 24:3-4 "By wisdom a house is built, and through understanding it is established; through knowledge its rooms are filled with rare and beautiful treasures."

What a powerful picture to study—our leadership shaped and implemented by our skills and choices. In the previous passage, the word knowledge refers to truth. Therefore, we had better be well-grounded in the "truth."

To lead in our ever-changing and complex world requires a sequence of ready, aim, and then fire. We may have to do this rapidly since there is such a premium on speed, but the sequence is still true. We no longer are firing a musket, but an automatic weapon. If misfired or aimed incorrectly, it can cause devastation, collateral damage, or at a minimum, loss of time in correcting our mistake.

Some years ago, I had the opportunity to learn how to race Formula Fords. I attended an executive workshop called Yungah. It used the racing car as a metaphor for change. Each morning the Skip Barber Racing School Team would teach us what we needed to know about the car, racing, safety, and execution on the track. In the afternoon, we would spend the time examining the applications to our businesses. It proved to be a very informative and fun experience.

There were three lessons that have stayed with me from that time to the present. First, you must unlearn to learn—and that is painful and difficult. Second, since all the cars are governed at 116 mph, the race is won on the curves, not the straightaways. It was the "slow" part of the race that required more discipline, skill, and understanding. It was also the part of the race that determined the winner. Third and finally, the driver—not the car—made the difference.

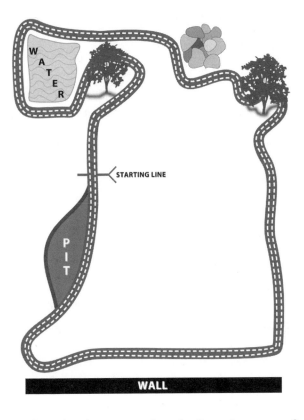

The leader who does not value the "go slow to go fast" phenomenon will cut short his preparation and investment at this stage. He may make a big splash to begin with, but will seldom be present at the finish line. This effort requires a thought process that is focused, an assessment of our resources, the right selection of these resources, persistence to the goals, and dedication to staying the course.

While there are likely more than five steps to Aiming for Perfection, the following are too critical to our success as a leader to leave out of our conscious focus.

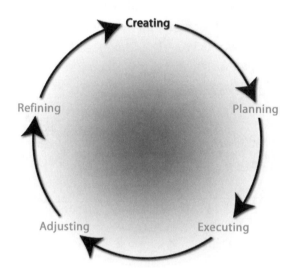

CREATING

For many of you, it will appear that the first step should be planning and then creating to the plan. The problem is that once a plan is on paper or in our head, our creativity is limited. We have already established a framework or boundary for our creation. Again, The Perfect Leader is an appropriate reference for this sequence.

> Genesis 1:1 "In the beginning God created the heavens and earth."

Do we need to plan? Absolutely, but not first. Few things are as rewarding and challenging as the act of creating. People get excited, motivated, and involved during the creating phase. In my years of consulting, it has come to my attention just how seldom we empower our people or ourselves to create. To a large degree, it has become a lost art due to atrophy. It has been replaced with reactive problem solving—leading to a culture of crisis management. We begin to reward the person who can put out fires well ahead of the person who can prevent fires.

What would have happened if General Tommy Franks, our commander in the Iraqi Freedom War, had used the same tactics employed in World War II, Vietnam, or even the 1990 Gulf War? He took a lot of abuse initially for his "creative" new warfighting scheme. However, the casualties of our troops were at an unbelievably low number. It was a creation that started the strategy, not a plan.

Think of the last time you were involved in a creation—perhaps it was a house, a vacation, or a baby. Regardless of the creative purpose, it challenges us at our inner most being. I have often thought the creation of our business was more fun and exciting than the actual formation and incorporation. Obviously, a fire had been lit, and a new creation needed to come into play. This new creation became our vision (next chapter).

If creating is really this important and this much fun, then why is it so hard? I have already discussed one of the common causes; we have stopped expecting and rewarding people to be creative. For many of us, our last creation was the blue tree with purple leaves; then we were told by a well-meaning teacher that trees are brown and leaves are green. We should be more careful next time; to get an "A" on our paper, we must stay within the lines.

The other reason, my experience teaches me, is we stay too conventional in our concern about what others will think. This thinking translates to worry and anxiety about our acceptance, approval, recognition, and power. This does not mean we should spend our focus on trying to become creative with a devil-may-care-attitude. We must understand the business we play in and the industry that is attached to it. However, it does speak to the fact that it is often easier to go with the flow than to think outside the norm and see the possibility. Who among us is not familiar with the slogan "better safe than sorry"?

How different our world would be if Henry Ford had decided not to risk the ridicule of his horseless carriage. Instead, he went about creating a vehicle that has been a mainstay for jobs, wealth, and industrial development for more than a hundred years.

Allow me to give you a tantalizer for chapter four on Value Based Character. As leaders, we can challenge this type of thinking. One of DLPA's values tells our staff that they should "err on the side of action." We expect, reward, and recognize creative action not mental stagnation.

During the 1996 NFL Draft, Jimmy Johnson, the new coach of the Miami Dolphins, was asked to defend his controversial, first-round selection of Baylor's Darrel Gardner. He stated, "As you know I'm not too concerned what others think. I think this player has the most upside potential in the draft. He has the ability to be a dominating player in the NFL."

At the conclusion of the interview, ESPN's Joe Theismann said, "What a lucky player Darrel Gardner is to get drafted by Jimmy Johnson." Why? Because his coach is into creating All-Pro players and Super Bowl champions. Check his record; many other coaches took a much more conventional route and likely drafted a safer, if less potential, player. Seven years later, Jimmy Johnson was right, and Darrel Gardner is an All-Pro *and* a rich man.

The formula for creating could easily be *wisdom (skills) X understanding (choices) X knowledge (truth)*.

Applied creativity = W x U x K

Example: W (Jimmy Johnson's skill at developing players) x U (choosing a player with potential) x K (Gardner's performance record at Baylor) = Creative Selection

Having the "truth," information, or facts is significantly different from being able to discern the application, circumstance, and judgment necessary to apply the "truth."

Notice my formula is using multiplication signs and not addition signs. Therefore, if one is missing, the formula is zero—no applied creativity.

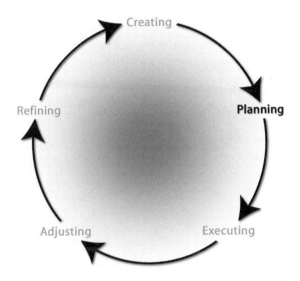

PLANNING

For many of us, the more inclined we are to create, the less inclined we are to plan in detail. Winston Churchill said, "Plans never work but planning is everything." The act of planning helps the leader examine a logically thought-out

Rollout of his initiative. With this documentation, consider the impact of outside and internal factors on the activity. I personally find the act of planning to be more beneficial than the plan itself in most circumstances. This is likely due to the complexity of the business environment and the frequent changes one must respond to in order to stay current.

Be careful that the plan does not become the end in itself or *the* answer to how a goal can be achieved. The great leader remains flexible and uses the plan as a guideline and benchmark as to the desired cost and time allotment. The plan also can serve as a framework, giving structure and order to those expected to execute the activities.

The Perfect Leader had a plan for mankind. This plan incorporated the free-will bestowed upon Adam and Eve. This plan was enacted as Adam and Eve went outside the boundary of the plan and rules (Genesis Chapter 1).

Planning helps us to stay proactive and on schedule as we respond to the necessary adjustments brought about by our strengths, weaknesses, threats, and resources within our span of control. This thought process helps us respond from a point of preparation and not panic.

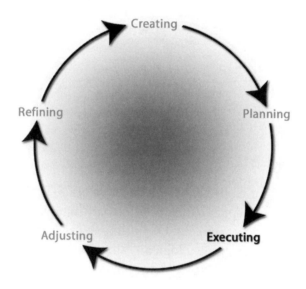

EXECUTING

Creating and planning are done to help the execution. Execution is what it is all about. Do we win or lose, produce or fail, compete or go bankrupt? Execution is often the fun phase of aiming for perfection. It is the one phase that is on display for all to see and evaluate. It becomes the scorecard by which we can compare our performance to the standard we set during the creating and planning process.

In my opinion, this ability separates the best leaders from the rest of the field. Even when his creation and plans are not works of art, the great leader adjusts and makes lemonade out of lemons.

In our society, action is highly valued and rewarded; it is worth emphasizing that action without the first two phases is seldom sustainable. Plus, execution alone is very hard to understand and follow without the creation and plan.

While there are many factors that assist or interfere with effective execution, I will briefly highlight five of these. (Reference the following chapters to gain greater insights into major issues affecting execution: courage, versatility, and empowerment.)

A leader must be available in order to guide, to direct, and to provide the necessary support and coaching to his people. In the absence of the leader, the employee tends to wait and then provide his own answers or get his answers from other coworkers. If this is a routine or simple assignment, it likely is low-risk. Likewise, if the employee group is very mature and experienced, the risk is lower. However, the converse is also true. New assignments, complex assignments, or inexperienced coworkers require a leader to be readily available.

It should be noted that while technology such as e-mail and voice mail can increase contact, it is no replacement for face-to-face contact. No request is more prevalent in the workforce today than the desire to have more contact with the leader.

The Perfect Leader once again gives us the model. After every significant new lesson He teaches or demonstrates, we observe Him spending time with his followers. During this time, He is debriefing and coaching, and the real learning and application is transferred from leader to follower. (Mark 6:30–52 is a good example.)

A leader must also be decisive in order to keep the execution phase moving toward its conclusion. If the leader keeps in mind the goal, the impact on the people, the mission, the vision of the organization, and finally, the team's principles, then a decision should be easily made within this framework. A leader may wonder or have doubts. *By the time I check all of these factors, it will take forever.* This is true if the above factors are only for show and not etched in the leader's mind and heart. If these factors are part of your leadership persona, then all these factors are a conscious part of every action the leader takes and every decision he makes.

Execution to accomplish a significant task or goal nearly always requires other people to be involved. This frequently becomes a team in today's business environment. The Perfect Leader formed a team in order to achieve the far-reaching targets of his vision. He continued to add members to this team as his purpose was fulfilled and the expected results expanded.

Two cautions warrant a heads-up. First, the leader must be willing to relinquish some of his control in order to keep the execution phase on task. The exception is when he is the only person capable (the sole expert). This should lead to a conscious development opportunity for a follower, or the leader will always be required to fill this role, thus relegating himself to doer versus leader.

When the leader over controls the information, activity, or people, the outcome is retarded development and over dependence upon the leader. Some popular literature refers to this type of leader as a "heroic leader."

Finally, an effective leader understands that his followers are different and must be dealt with according to their unique motivations, strengths, and weaknesses. This requires consistency and fairness from the leader, complimented by a more tailored delivery. (The best training I have been exposed to for this skill set is a program developed by Wilson Learning called Social Style Management.)

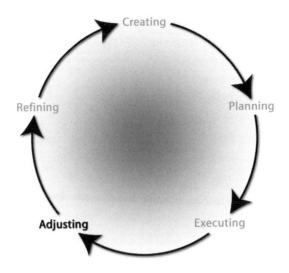

ADJUSTING

Have you noticed the great coaches in college and professional sports usually win the last half of the game? They use the halftime break to modify their original plan. They review the team's demonstrated first half execution against what the opponent is doing. This ability and willingness to adjust is frequently what separates the champion from the runner-up.

Few plans are executed as designed, and even fewer actually work as planned. It has always amazed me that while we list planning as one of the basic five skills a manager must possess, adjusting lacks any recognition at all. If few plans work as devised, the leader must develop the skills to adjust quickly. The skills require an ability to concentrate on the action, interpret what was observed, and communicate the required change needed to the player or employee.

The skill set for the twenty-first-century leader should involve adjusting and increasing agility, just as evolutionary skills were to the twentieth-century leader, who specialized in planning and control.

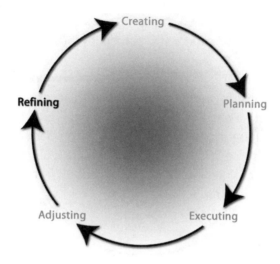

REFINING

Adjusting is frequently an on-the-spot response and initiated in order to keep the execution phase moving forward. While it is very similar to refining, adjusting is a separate skill and all too often a short-term focus. The adjustments become the basis for improving the next execution on a permanent level.

Refining is the exercise that allows this learning to be implemented and begins the process of continuous improvement toward perfection. We cannot "Aim for Perfection" if we are unable to observe the execution's successes and failures. Then we must adjust and refine.

The Perfect Leader gives us a reference to the development of his people in Zechariah 13:9.

> "This third I will bring into the fire; I will refine them like silver and test them like gold. They will call on my name and I will answer them; I will say, 'They are my people,' and they will say, 'The Lord is our God.' "

Even The Perfect Leader acknowledges that many will

refuse development. Two-thirds rejected his leadership in this passage. Should we expect 100 percent of our charges to change or adapt?

Aiming for perfection gives the leader an opportunity to set a high standard, to set the expectations for everyone involved, and to set forth a challenge for each person to give his best. This creates a lifelong journey toward excellence. A constant adjusting and refining of our leadership behavior is equivalent to being in the fire; our skills, knowledge, and attitudes are the gold and silver that is being refined.

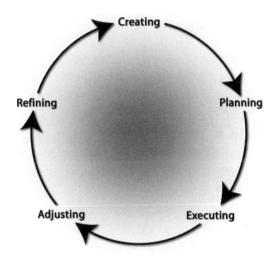

AVOID BEING A PERFECTIONIST

"Aim for Perfection" does not mean to be a perfectionist. Aiming is the process, not the result. I do not know one great leader who is a perfectionist. However, many perfectionists think they are great leaders.

Why not be a perfectionist? There are many reasons that this trait gets in the way of leadership, and this chapter will review a few of them. Several reasons come to the forefront.

A perfectionist is very difficult to satisfy; therefore, his communication tends to come across to the follower as being overly critical and nitpicky. If the goal is perfection, then anything that is not perfect must be challenged, confronted, and changed. Few people are motivated to follow someone who always tells them what is wrong and never seems to be pleased or satisfied with the effort.

The Perfect Leader continually challenges us to improve and never to settle for less than our best effort. Reality says few things must be perfect, but nearly all processes and products need to improve. The same is true of people.

> Colossians 3:23 "Whatever you do, work at it with all your heart, as working for the Lord, not men."

The Perfect Leader wants us to improve. We can observe his example throughout the New Testament as He challenges, teaches, and mentors his followers. He encourages them as progress is made, and He builds within them a desire to improve while validating their self-worth. This self-esteem translates into better performance and a willingness to take more risk, more responsibility, and more accountability.

A second reason to avoid the perfectionist style is the unreal expectations that it places on the leader and his followers.

Knowing our people and their limitations (at this exact time in their current development cycle) is a critical attribute of a leader. In fact, my experience working with leaders in my consulting role has taught me an unexpected lesson. An effective leader is often more accurately aware of a person's potential and his current limitations than the person is of his own status.

This phenomenon was particularly true of The Perfect Leader. What other leader would have called his "leaders to be" from a group as diverse, inexperienced, and young as the disciples. He was able to see beyond the physical, raw talent of these young people and focus on their attitude, willingness, and commitment. However, raw talent without leadership and guidance would only result in a confused and marginally successful individual.

Raw talent might make good, gung-ho kamikaze pilots, but the result is fatal. The drill sergeant, who is required to develop the raw recruit into a battle-savvy soldier, is a critical part toward the battle being won and the soldier's survival.

> I Samuel 16:7 " . . . The Lord does not look at the things man looks at. Man looks at the outward appearance, but the Lord looks at the heart."

The Perfect Leader enrolled fishermen, tax collectors, prostitutes, beggars, and business people to name a few "careers" and caused them to want to follow Him. He caused them to grow and change. He caused them to raise their standards. He caused them to believe in themselves. He caused them to become leaders in their own right. He caused them to aim for perfection.

It is no surprise that long after his death and resurrection, his followers became the leaders, the leaders to carry his vision forward. These followers, now the leaders, developed their followers into leaders, and so the cycle continued.

The third reason to resist being a perfectionist is because it is the wrong goal.

If the goal were to do things perfectly or to be perfect in our leadership behavior, we would never get around to many of our initiatives or finish many activities. The Perfect Leader was a man of action. As leaders, we need to know when expectations are met with the required quality and move on to other challenges.

The world of the twenty-first-century leader is too complex, ambiguous, and changing to expect perfection in many things. The goal is to continue to improve, learn, and take action. Once again, this is not an excuse to do less than what we are capable of delivering.

The following passage endorses the emphasis The Perfect Leader puts on continuing to improve, to learn, and to take action. Note, it does not indicate that we should wait to move to the next characteristic until we can master the current one perfectly. If it did, we would never get past the first step.

> II Peter 1:5–8 "For this very reason, make every effort to add to your faith goodness; and to goodness knowledge; and to knowledge self-control; and to self-control, perseverance; and to perseverance, godliness; and to godliness, brotherly kindness; and to brotherly kindness, love. For if you possess these qualities in increasing measure, they will keep you from being ineffective and unproductive in your knowledge of our Lord Jesus Christ."

The fourth point to make concerning perfectionism is that it is overkill. In my years of consulting with such companies as General Electric, Lockheed Martin, Libbey Glass, and Sandia National Laboratories, to name a few, I have come to understand and appreciate the term "minimal acceptable standard."

In other words, a customer or user has, through diligent research, determined the degree to which his product should perform. Does this mean it is of quality? Absolutely yes! It explains to the contractor that going above this standard will show no appreciable gain, will increase cost, and likely defer delivery due to excess time being put into the process. The goal is not perfection but a reliable, well-performing product.

Had The Perfect Leader waited until Peter had a perfect temperament or Paul perfected his aggressiveness or Andrew became assertive enough or Thomas became a positive thinker, then we would never have seen any action come from these followers. The goal is to get better every day, building on our strengths.

The fifth and final point to ponder regarding perfectionism is that it is neither effective nor efficient.

In a time when competition is fierce, we must be aware of any wasted time, dollars, or energy. The perfectionist does not lead in this manner, but requires too much detail at the cost of speed. It frequently creates a C.Y.A. attitude among the followers, which results in the doers feeling angry, insecure, and negative.

To the leader, this focus leads to delayed decisions and even paralysis by analysis. The purpose has been lost in the process.

READY, AIM, FIRE

Now that the goal is clearly in the leader's sight, it is time to pull the trigger and begin the pursuit of the prize. The following chapters will describe the attributes and characteristics of perfect leadership as validated by the approach demonstrated by The Perfect Leader.

If you are applying this format to your business, my suggestion is to use the next three chapters in a progressive sequence. Establish your vision, determine your mission, and define your values/principles.

By doing this, you will have focus and the decision triangle that will allow you to be a decisive and dynamic leader. The fun is about to begin.

CHAPTER TWO

THE PERFECT LEADER QUALITY #2:
VISION DRIVEN

"For where there is no vision, the people perish."
Proverbs 29:18 (KJV)

What a staggering thought. You mean that because I have not spent time articulating and picturing what I want the future to look like for my business that this simple oversight could result in my company's bankruptcy? Could it contribute to my follower's unemployment? Could it contribute to my customer's demise? The answer according to The Perfect Leader is yes, yes, and yes.

Wait a minute. Since when did this "soft measurement" become such a strategic and critical leadership criteria? I think we could make a strong case that The Perfect Leader established this in the first verse of the Bible.

Genesis 1:1 begins the Creation chapter. Why was all of this creating taking place? What was the picture supposed to look like when it was complete, and who was it all for? Genesis 1:27–31 paints the picture (vision) of what was to take place. Mankind was to have a good place to live, food to eat, and a positive environment in which to raise families. The entire activity started with the outcome in mind. All of this had a purpose and direction. It was imperative to see the vision in order to create and develop the necessary plan.

After twenty-three years in consulting and training within

the context of organizational change, I believe there are four major reasons why so many of today's so-called leaders fail to be vision driven. A brief summary:

1. They are so caught up in the tyranny of the urgent that the strategically important points are ignored.

2. Many of today's most senior management are from the "old school." Since it is difficult to measure "vision" progress, they are more comfortable with the old, traditional approach—variations of management by objectives that measure primarily progress on tasks and goals. Either they don't want to get the necessary training to be current in the field of management and leadership, or they are afraid to. Why would I use the reference of fear? If I am deficient of a skill and the training exposes this deficiency, I must learn and change.

    Change is frequently uncomfortable, and to the person who has been rewarded as successful and has the "title" to prove it, he has much vested in the old way. Simple questions arise within him, *Will I lose credibility while I'm learning? Will I be as successful with this new approach?*

    Ecclesiastes 10:10 "If the ax is dull and its edge unsharpened, more strength is needed, but skill will bring success."

3. The saddest of all the reasons is one that most leaders will deny or challenge. Plain and simple, there is a lack of courage. Guts are required if we are truly vision driven. A major study into organizational initiatives validated that at the onset of the strategy, a full 25 percent of the employees are "open naysayers."

This means they are verbally fighting and bad-mouthing the prescribed change.

Vision cannot happen without the leader's full commitment and the courage to see it through.

The United States business community is great at pursuing the latest trend. Is vision one of these trends? No. In fact, any significant accomplishment in life began with a vision of a desired outcome (a clear picture hoped for in the mind's eye) long before the action to accomplish this effort began. Do you have the courage, skills, confidence, and faith to create and communicate a vision for your business and its employees?

You can count on the fact that some key people will likely not make the transition and become casualties. They will miss the opportunity to be a part of the future by hanging on too long to the past.

It will be risky since the future is not certain, maybe even a little dreamy to your followers. It will certainly cause debate, criticism, and doubt about your leadership. Maybe we should just wait a little longer, and then the timing will be right. After all, the future will take care of itself, won't it? You are the leader, or you would not be the one reading this book. It is really **your call.** Will you allow the people to perish?

"From the moment CEO Michael Spindler assumed leadership and proudly announced that vision wasn't his thing, it was clear that he was a perverse choice to lead a company perpetually lodged on the hip leading edge. Vision is the sort of quality that leads one to observe a looming avalanche called the Internet (the global computer network that's changing everything), and position the company to ski above it. Instead, Apple launched its dismal proprietary eWorld system, while upstart Netscape took Apple's place as King on the Valley . . ."[1]

This article could have been written about any number of bosses who are now extinct. In addition, this application can be true of organizations, people, careers, skills, countries, churches, businesses, etc.

The more successful you are now, the more this chapter should serve as a challenge and wake-up call. We are all inclined to leave what is working alone. Success feels good and frequently creates apathy about trying to improve upon it. How many times have you heard the American battle cry, *If it ain't broken, don't fix it?* That is not a quote from a leader, but from a dinosaur in the making.

If history has taught us anything, it has shown us that everything will break. Could the breakage be due to the leader's focus on the past and present? If so, this creates a blind spot of the future. The people perish, the business perishes, and the leader perishes. Was it due to ignorance, arrogance, oversight, lack of courage, lack of skill, or complacency? Regardless, failure is failure; leadership was on vacation.

Make sure to read the previous paragraph again, and be sure of its meaning. The context is an attitude, not that successes should not be repeated.

All of us are in this game to be successful. However, success can give us a false sense of security and lull us into complacency and rationalization. Even world champion teams modify their personnel before the next season; those that don't almost never repeat as champions.

Change is uncomfortable, but it is as certain as death and taxes. As Peter Drucker said, "The best way to predict the future is to create it." The Perfect Leader says to develop a vision and help the people flourish.

DEFINITION

Vision is defined as a detailed, intense picture of a realistic, credible, attractive future and a condition significantly better in important ways to its participants than what currently exists.

By definition and usage, vision incorporates a broad range of concepts such as foresight, discernment, imagination, and even dreaming. Webster's describes vision as "a manifestation to the senses of something immaterial." In other words, vision involves both the visible and invisible worlds. It takes what is unseen, the realm of hopes, goals, dreams, and aspirations and makes them tangible in the visible world in which we live.

Vision is the ability to see. Vision does not merely see what will or might be; it also sees what was and what is. How leaders and their organizations view the future is directly and powerfully influenced by how they view both the past and the present. Vision will help us to see the consequences (both positive and negative), processes, products, and solutions to keep us competitive.

It is from this leadership tool (vision) that we can begin the process of seeing how things can be better (and different) in the future AND what must be done to secure that future.

PURPOSE OF VISION

One thing, of which I am certain, is that The Perfect Leader creates order, not chaos. Therefore, any principle or approach He takes is designed to provide order and validate the faith of his followers.

Stress is a relatively new term to mankind. We have certainly embraced this term as a major reason for all kinds of problems facing business and its affect on outcomes. In recent years we have all become familiar with the rapidity of change and the ambiguity and complexity it brings. Put these two factors together, and we can have chaos.

Research in the social sciences indicates that people can handle incredible degrees of change and stress if two elements exist for the individual. The elements are hope and support.

Vision serves to provide the "hope" for its participants.

In addition, vision serves as the first step in creating organizational alignment. Once a vision (future direction) is determined, communication can begin in order to create a meaning and reward for its participants. Once the vision is established, the leader can then align the organization's mission, strategies, goals, roles, and responsibilities.

In other words, the leader is following the model of The Perfect Leader. He is creating order for his followers and ultimately providing a path through the changing world. The result? Less chaos, more focus with less stress. The people have hope.

The leader who is courageous enough to create and communicate his vision has addressed the challenge of Proverbs 29:18. It could read for them: *Where there is vision the people have hope and prosper.*

QUALITIES OF AN EFFECTIVE VISION

There are several qualities that a vision must address in order to be credible and motivating to its participants. It is appropriate at this time to emphasize that a vision or vision statement is a tool to be used internally. It is for the members of the organization, not its customers. On occasion, it could be appropriate to share this with your customers, but don't expect the customer to be excited or focused because of the vision. At times, it may help in establishing strategic alliances, but this is the exception not the rule.

1.   A vision must be a tangible picture of the future environment. The picture should be as clear as holding a Polaroid in your hand. If you can't see it, you can't create it.

2.   A vision must explicitly include all its stakeholders. If my photo is not visibly evident in the picture, then I will feel excluded in the future the leader is trying to create.

Life's lessons are all too often taught to us by the youngest and most innocent teachers. Years ago, my youngest daughter Dawn came into our family room, picked up a family album from our coffee table, and climbed into my lap.

At 4 years of age, this was one of those special moments, one to cherish as she cuddled in my arms and began to turn the pages of our family album. We had only two children at that time, and Dawn and her older sister Kim were our treasures.

As Dawn turned the pages, she began to point and call out the names of the people familiar to her. Then she turned to numerous pictures of a baby. She would say, "That is me."

I would say, "No, Honey. That is Kim." This went on for several pages; then, without warning, she climbed down from my lap, put the album back on the table, and without a word, went into another room.

Dawn had fallen victim to the second-child-picture syndrome. This is the syndrome where only grandparents take pictures of the second kid; the parents are either too preoccupied or too broke.

Besides breaking my heart, I experienced a lifelong lesson. Pictures have no interest if we are not in the pictures. The leader who creates a vision and excludes a person from seeing himself in the future picture has erred. The excluded person will have no more motivation to create that future than you or I would be motivated to see a stranger's home movies.

3. The vision must be created by leaders. While it does not have to be created by a single person, it must be owned and driven by leadership. If a team is the leader, all must be enlisted in creating the vision.

The cartoon character Pogo had an interesting way to describe becoming a leader. He suggested to find a parade and get in front of it! To the contrary, leaders are the parade makers.

It is the leader who sees the potential of an idea or a way to create a competitive advantage or a challenge to be embraced that could spell the difference between winning and losing. The leader owns the vision and its installation. Once installed, the leader must continue to enroll and recruit members to its cause. He must do this often, as followers tend to believe messages we repeat often and not the ones that are seldom mentioned. We have trained them in this phenomenon. Take any measurement or message that is critical to our success and we talk about it frequently, any and every chance we get. We link it to every possible event, meeting, etc. So why would our followers believe the vision is important if we do not discuss it at any and every opportunity we have?

The leader must demonstrate his commitment to the achievement of the vision. As a follower, I must know the leader will not compromise his ethical pursuit of its outcome. This includes the tough calls when it comes to personnel, resources, and finances.

Whether we agree with President George W. Bush or not, he has created a compelling vision of a United States without terrorism. Each of us can envision how it affects us and what it will look like when it is achieved. On the other hand, it is easy to see how France, Germany, and the rest of the world can so easily criticize the actions the vision requires. After all, it is not their vision; it is not their family album. Their leaders have lacked the courage to stop terrorism; thus, their countries can only criticize and blame our stand and our actions. Is it any surprise that even in a miserable economic climate his personal approval rating grew by over twenty percentage points?

If a vision is created by leaders, then how do we get the followers committed? The key is to help them see the benefit and excitement of the vision, and then allow them to participate in how the vision will be achieved. This is involvement at its highest level, requiring the employees to use their skills, knowledge, and attitudes. For them, it is a creation, a chance to shape their future and security.

4.	The vision must be attainable, credible, and motivating. You may have noticed that the word used is attainable and not realistic. In many situations, the vision of the leader is too great a stretch for the people to see it as realistic. This is typical because the basis for realism is in what now exists and is known. Attainable may still be doubted, but it brings a question of the unknown with it. So it is evaluated differently.

Credible simply requires the vision to be believable and worthy of the effort. To be motivating to the stakeholders, the vision must offer something of benefit—first to the individual and then to the organization. The weaknesses of many vision statements are that they clearly present how the *organization* gains through the effort, but it is left to the imagination as to what is in it for the people. To be motivating, it must be worth my time, effort, and energy. I must see personal gain of some sort.

I can remember hearing President Kennedy share his vision of landing a man on the moon in a ten-year time frame. I am sure there were many smirks, jokes, and doubts concerning his challenge to the nation. It was not realistic for most of us, but it was potentially attainable if we could martial the resources and energy of our people. It was definitely motivating for those of us wanting to stay ahead of the Russians and continue our way of life. Finally, based on our history of meeting challenges and the track record of our scientific successes, it was credible.

5. The vision must be tangible enough to serve as a decision-making tool. Once the vision is developed and a strategy and plan for its achievement have been established, then we must make our decisions with the vision in mind. If our proposed activity does not move us toward the vision or help align our stakeholders, then a decision should be made to rework our activity. As The Perfect Leader demonstrated, all his activities were in alignment with his vision, mission, and values.

6. Vision requires action. In his video, *The Power of Vision,* Joel Barker, futurist and author, makes a very good and accurate observation. "Vision without action is but a dream. Vision with action can change the universe."[2]

When a leader creates a vision and then does not give it his total commitment or fails to move it to action, then the leader has committed a fatal flaw. Not only is the vision going to remain a "dream," but the leader will suffer untold criticism and loss of credibility. It would have been better for the leader to have kept his vision to himself than to have lacked the courage to pursue and support it.

The Perfect Leader gives direction in this endeavor as well. Ecclesiastes 5:4–6 gives us a clear message about following through on our verbal commitments. While our visions may not have been to God, the verses give us a great leadership characteristic. Be honest, keep our word, and don't try to talk our way out of what we acted our way into.

> Ecclesiastes 5:4–6 "When you make a vow to God, do not delay in fulfilling it. He has no pleasure in fools; fulfill your vow. It is better not to vow than to make a vow and not fulfill it. Do not let your mouth lead you into sin. And do not protest to the temple messenger, "My vow was a mistake.""

THE PERFECT LEADER'S VISION

If vision is a leadership competency we should pursue, then it would require that The Perfect Leader would have a vision. I do not pretend to know his exact vision. It appears to me that the following passage articulates his vision. It is a picture of what is possible with all stakeholders involved and what they can create together.

Matthew 28:18-20 Then Jesus came to them and said, "Therefore go and make disciples of all nations, baptizing them in the name of the Father and of the Son and of the Holy Spirit, and teaching them to obey everything I have commanded you. And surely I will be with you always, to the very end of the age."

Since I believe this to be the vision, let us examine this against the criteria established under Qualities of an Effective Vision.

1. Does it present a visible and tangible picture?
2. Could any stakeholder find himself in the vision?
3. Was it created by the leader?
4. Is it attainable, credible, and motivating?
5. Does it provide a basis for making decisions?
6. Has the vision created action?

Once the basic qualifying questions have been answered, we can offer a few additional questions.

Have you as the leader actively enrolled, persuaded, and solicited followers to your vision?

Have you provided the training, coaching, and mentoring required to execute the vision?

Are you visibly leading the effort?

For two thousand years, The Perfect Leader's vision has served to motivate its stakeholders. The vision has spread to every nation in the world, validating that it is attainable, credible, and motivational. The Perfect Leader created and provided, through his other teachings, a framework for decision-making. Obviously, the number of stakeholders increase everyday and put themselves into the picture. Finally, it has created action to pursue its achievement.

Notice this was not a vision created by his disciples, his followers, the experts at the temples, or anyone else. At this point in time, they were not the leaders responsible for establishing this challenge. They may have been leaders in other professions (in their own tasks), but not in this vision.

To make the vision move toward reality, The Perfect Leader began to enroll, persuade, and solicit followers to enlist in his vision. As these followers were trained, coached, and mentored in the ways of this vision, they began to act in ways to help with its implementation. They began to be involved with how achievement was to occur. In time, they began to grow into leadership roles themselves.

The heritage had started. From follower, to involvement, to leadership, this process has been active for two thousand years. The Perfect Leader's vision is alive and well.

I have learned many lessons from The Perfect Leader's example and vision. Two are of particular importance to me as a twenty-first-century leader.

Lesson one: Never measure the situation by the current resources. This is likely a book in itself; put simply, have faith in your vision and get involved in its action. Opportunity will be presented to those who are prepared.

> Ephesians 5:15–16 "Be very careful, then, how you live - not as unwise but as wise, making the most of every opportunity . . ."

Lesson two: Focus precedes success. Anything that requires a concentrated effort is first visualized in our minds if we are to be successful. Vision provides the focus for the twenty-first-century leader.

To put these lessons to the test, read The Perfect Leader's approach and actions in the feeding of the five thousand (Mark 6:30–42).

CHAPTER THREE

PERFECT LEADER QUALITY #3:
ALIGNED ON PURPOSE

*Jesus replied, "Let us go somewhere else - to the
nearby villages - so I can preach there also.
That is why I have come."*

Mark 1:38

If you are short of people, need a boost in productivity, and want an immediate boost in morale–pay attention. This chapter is for you. It will be easy to understand, but difficult to do. Not because the concepts and skills are rocket science, but because we will be required to make hard decisions, force change, and lead through our mission statement.

We live in a society where it appears we need thirty hours in every day. The problem is that if we had the thirty hours, we would not get much more accomplished. We would be more exhausted, more confused, and wish more than ever that we had thirty-six hours in a day! No wonder it is reported that we have in excess of 30 million sleep-deprived citizens in the United States!

During the last six years our staff has conducted many team building workshops and strategic planning sessions. We have discovered a factor that is costing American businesses untold millions, not to say anything about the impact on its other resources. Easily, 20 percent of the day-to-day work that people are hired to complete takes a backseat to activities that are non-value added.

In other words, we are spending much of our time, energy, and resources chasing activities and tasks outside our mission. It has little or no pay-off, yet continues daily and robs us of our focus and productivity. The astonishing fact is that when brought to the leader's attention, seldom is anything changed. Even the people doing the work would rather talk about it than do anything about it. This would be equivalent to the Dallas Cowboys spending part of every practice shooting baskets with the coaches, and the players knowing that it has nothing to do with football.

The most amazing quality of The Perfect Leader is that He was always on his personal purpose while fulfilling his organizational mission. Therefore, He wasted no resources, time, energy, or attitude for either Himself or his followers—efficiency and effectiveness that any leader would cherish to model.

In the Mark 1:38 passage, He made a difficult choice. His disciples needed Him, and everyone else was looking for Him according to verse 37. Being a person that loved people, couldn't he do both? Not if He stayed on purpose and accomplished his purpose in the three short years He was given. The choice and decision was determined by his mission.

I would have likely tried to do both; I would work the people in for a few minutes, and then I would try to speed to the next assignment. I would then feel rushed, interrupted, frustrated with my limited time, and be off-purpose. If I did this two or three times a day, I would feel over-committed and stressed, in need of the 36-hour day. My purposeful work put off to completion until tomorrow.

This is not to imply that The Perfect Leader was a workaholic or preferred preaching to people. He made time to spend with his friends, to rest and relax, to go to parties, and to have his quiet times. He had time to do this because He stayed on purpose, and this focus created adequate space for the other events.

The absence of purpose and mission as an understood and dynamic leadership tool is missing in most work units that I have encountered. Many of them accomplish great goals. The consequence usually shows up over time, taking the form of burnout, confusion, loss of teamwork, or just not having fun anymore.

With my background as an athlete and coach, it was very clear to me that our basketball team did not need five point guards, and the baseball team did not need nine shortstops. Each player had a purpose. When the players performed on purpose, we were almost always successful. When we did not, the advantage went to the competition.

Nearly every business or organization has a mission statement. The problem is, too few know how to use it.

MISSION AND PURPOSE DEFINED

Mission and purpose are in many ways synonymous. "Mission" is usually used in terms to reference a business or work unit. "Purpose" is the term used to describe the individual's focus.

Mission is defined as the reason for existence. It is the unique function the business or work unit has established to provide to its customer. When looking at the macro view of the organization, it defines the business we are in.

Every department and every work unit, having their own missions, provide the micro view. Technically, each mission statement is unique but supportive and aligned to the organization's mission. Duplication of the same mission will result in replication of the same work, identifying one work unit that is unnecessary.

When a work group is unclear on its mission or has a mission that is underutilized, it always takes on work that provides little or no value. Other common symptoms include confusion on roles and responsibilities, impaired decision- making and long hours to do the required work to meet the original focus of the work unit.

My reason for existing is *my purpose*. That is its definition. I believe the work we do either helps or hinders the pursuit of our purpose. The people I've met who are the most fulfilled and satisfied by their work are the people whose work and purposes are aligned. The opposite is also true.

The Perfect Leader reflects this principle to Solomon.

> Ecclesiastes 2:24. "A man can do nothing better than to eat and drink and find satisfaction in his work . . ."

If work does not provide fulfillment, then we frequently job hunt or pursue this needed satisfaction through our off-hour activities. We all have this need; yet few people have taken the time to identify their purpose and develop a plan to achieve it.

Does everyone have a purpose and plan? The Perfect Leader tells us in Jeremiah 29:11 — the answer is yes.

> "For I know the plans I have for you," declares the Lord, "plans to prosper you and not to harm you, plans to give you hope and a future."

Although we would like to think prosper means financial gain, it likely means personal growth.

As employers, we would be much wiser in our hiring practices if we took time to help our current staff identify its "purpose fit" within our organization and helped identify the underlying purposes of prospective employees. Turnovers, poor performances, lack of task energy, and off-purpose activities all have a strong correlation — we have just never taken the time or money to research and validate these factors to meet today's paradigm.

The Perfect Leader was aligned. His purpose and mission were synchronized with the work He was to perform and the goals He was to achieve. His mission was to save (John 3:17); his purpose was to teach and preach (Mark 1:38).

Our purpose will take advantage of and utilize our talents, skills, and knowledge. Feeling underutilized or frustrated with not using our "God-given talents" is frequently the result of being off-purpose. Another major cause for this frustration is the organization failing to allow us to use our talents. Talents differ from learned skills in that they are easier for us to apply and demonstrate. They provide a sense of worth when we can use them at work. They are our natural abilities.

ALIGNED ON PURPOSE

Today's literature frequently speaks of alignment. It touts the importance and value of creating an organization with all its people and work units being aligned. This leadership task is absolutely critical for the twenty-first-century leader and business. It is also one that The Perfect Leader modeled and endorsed.

The dictionary defines alignment as "arrangement in a straight line."

For the business leader, alignment is a continuous six-step cycle.

1. Create and document all components that make up organizational alignment. This means each work unit has all alignment components.
2. Be the first to set the example; get in front of the parade you are about to create.
3. Communicate daily what it is, why it is important, and examples where it has been used or ignored.
4. Train all employees.
5. Establish consequences to reward or punish.
6. Protect it with the authority and power given you— unconditional compromise. Any activity or person out of alignment must be confronted and a decision made to eliminate or realign.

Now that the steps have been established, what must we align? Alignment is accomplished when the vision of leadership, the organization's mission, strategies to achieve the mission, its goals, and the roles and responsibilities are "arranged in a straight line." When action is taken on any one of the components, it should result in a favorable impact on each of the other components. This is true alignment. For example, when a goal is achieved, our strategies to accomplish our mission become a reality.

When we add the fuel or life-blood to these components, action is eminent toward our future. The life-blood of the organization is our commonly held values and principles. (An entire chapter is dedicated to this leadership quality.)

Each of these components is a link in the chain, or in my model, a rung on the ladder. They are nothing without each other. They are complementary, supportive, enhancing, and synergistic with each other. When put together, they are the fundamentals behind a change system.

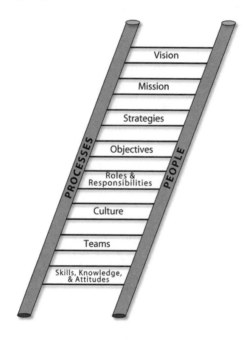

When we align these components and recruit the people to put them into action, we shape the culture of the organization. If we fail to create alignment, we also shape the culture!

Unfortunately, we have given birth, by our own omission, to an organization whose culture will provide inefficiencies, turf wars, lower morale, and impaired productivity on an all-too-frequent basis. Instead of focus and clarity, we have assisted in growing seeds of confusion and doubt within our midst.

Any significant change must consider organizational alignment.

Many of my clients have initially considered alignment a "nice to have" versus a "have to have" strategy. Once the school of hard knocks has validated the grief spent with people misaligned with you or that the cost of work units are in conflict with other departments, the issue of alignment is understood as the nonnegotiable factor that it is.

To require alignment of all components takes courage. A case-in-point that illustrates the courage required of leadership took place with one of our clients in the late 90's. **Mistake number one** was making an exception for one of the senior executive staff to name his own terms for playing on the executive team and not having to commit to promoting the vision and mission of the company. **Mistake number two** was failing to take a strong disciplinary action on a very successful manager that continued to second-guess and publicly criticize the direction and initiatives of the leadership team (of which he was a part). **Mistake number three** was not formally using the alignment components to recruit and train a key senior management hire. Thus the wrong person was hired, and many suffered as a result.

Employee morale went from high to very low. Employees wanted to know if senior management was still serious about its vision and values. They questioned if there was a double standard. The training they had been given to assist their efforts was reduced, and even the "endorsed training" began having a difficult time maintaining good attendance. A new "consulting guru" was hired. He had less than in-depth insight and accuracy and began passing judgment on the managers and supervisors. Employees and senior management divided as to which of two leaders was *the* leader and which message they should follow. Some good people left; many others checked out mentally. Productivity went down, and safety problems went up.

Many of the symptoms were difficult to see from an outsider's vantage point. The stock continued to perform adequately and profits were in line, but the foundation had serious cracks. When the problem was not addressed in a timely manner, the final chapter was written. This onetime industry leader was dying. It became just one of the many companies where nothing special or exciting was going on. In time, the cracks in the foundation became visible to the outside world. Executives were replaced; managers, supervisors and other employees were dismissed because the business was not performing to expectations. No one will be able to recall where the wrong turn was taken, or even that it happened over a three-year period. No one will pinpoint that it was a loss of purpose, mission, and alignment that essentially killed the vitality and specialness. No one will believe it started with a few simple alignment decisions, *but it did!* Precedent was set.

Unfortunately, this turned out to be a fatal mistake. The company was acquired; the executive was released. The few managers that survived became part of a very controlling parent corporation, and a once great company (one of the three best cultures I had ever worked with) had vanished.

Being off-purpose and out of alignment is unforgiving in today's business climate.

The right answer is simple to understand, but it is difficult to do. Uncompromising alignment is required, coupled with leadership courage to do the right thing.

THE PERFECT LEADER'S MISSION

Continuing with my premise that The Perfect Leader set the example of how we should lead, it is also critical to examine whether He had a mission. I believe we will find his mission in John 3:17.

"For God did not send his Son into the world to condemn the world, but to save the world through him."

The Perfect Leader was in alignment with who sent Him—God. He was given a mission to accomplish in order for the master plan to be successful. His mission was to save. His personal purpose was to preach and teach. Every component of the alignment ladder was in place and linked together.

The Perfect Leader is a Creator of order. The model is available for all of us to think about, learn from, and to apply to our own situation.

FUNCTIONS AND BENEFITS OF MISSION

A mission statement is simply a concise, written declaration of the organization's reason for existence. It helps your employees focus and helps define what service or product will be provided to your customer.

Several years ago, while consulting with a large, electric company, I was asked to help put a senior management team back on track. There was a good deal of infighting and battles over turf and alignment, and the tension was destroying the interpersonal relationships among the team members.

The senior vice president that brought me into the situation was in her office and was explaining the current situation to me. I mentioned that at its root cause there appeared to be an alignment problem and asked if I could see the department's Mission Statement.

"Oh, yes," she responded. "We have one. We spent a whole week up in the mountains at a retreat to develop it." She hesitated for a moment trying to decide where the statement was located and then went to the closet. Reaching up to the top shelf, she grabbed a binder. As she returned to her desk, she began wiping off the dust from the cover.

Before she had an opportunity to open and read the statement, I asked her to tell me what was written in the statement; she could not tell me.

To this team and this executive, the mission statement was an exercise to complete so they, too, would have a mission. It had no meaning and was of absolutely no use as a tool to utilize leading this department. Within three years this team lost five of its eight members, including the senior vice president.

The point is that most businesses and work units today have a mission statement. Most of the employees are aware of it and can actually reference it. Usually, they at least know where it is located. However, few know how to use it. It represents a "slogan" on the wall. The mission gives them little context for their daily activities and decisions and seldom is used to align their skills and motivators to the work. Leaders frequently forget to use mission as the strategic and tactical tool that it should be.

The benefits of using and understanding the mission statement are numerous. A few will be discussed next and should help to establish the importance of this critical leadership criterion.

I believe there are five major benefits that are provided by having, using, and understanding the mission at all levels of the organization.

1. Focus precedes success. Our mission statement provides the focus that is necessary for all of our people. It will clarify the business we are in, the products and services we can provide, and the market segment that we must target to compete successfully.

In the early eighties, De La Porte and Associates, Inc. was a struggling new business. I would try nearly anything to keep us afloat and buy more survival time. One of those apparent opportunities had just presented itself. The law had been changed concerning certain personnel policies, and it looked ripe to catch this window of opportunity with a seminar. We hustled to put together a brochure and recruit the necessary facilitator. We bought a mailing list, printed our brochures, and mailed over 14,000 of them. We sent it third-class mail to save a few dollars and targeted Albuquerque and El Paso, Texas. We had never worked El Paso, but it seemed a good way to enter a market—another "off-mission" decision.

To say the least, it was a disaster—both in time and money. We could hardly meet our current financial obligations, much less fund this brilliant "new opportunity."

A few months later we learned our bulk mail brochures had never left the post office until four or five weeks after Christmas. The workshop was the third week of January. We were not in the direct mail seminar business and had no understanding of its success factors or idiosyncrasies.

This became one of my most important leadership lessons, thanks to a client and now close friend, Knute Sorenson. While explaining to Knute how unfairly we had been treated in this event, he shared some profound advice. "Terry, you need to change your mission." When I asked half-heartedly what it should be, he volunteered, "If there is money in it, you're in it."

His comment pierced my heart and brain. What he was telling me was that I had lost focus and moved outside our mission, and I was playing a game I knew nothing about. I had allowed our all too few precious resources to be spent on something that was not aligned with our business. In fact, I had robbed it of critical time and energy. We had started our business with a clear purpose and had lost sight of the focus. Mission provides focus; focus precedes success. I failed to use this leadership tool and put our young business into an even more precarious position.

2.   Another major benefit of having a clear mission is that it provides a critical boundary for the employees of the organization. When an individual can clearly understand the purpose of the work unit, then limitations are easily set. Those things we pursue that support our mission are

appropriate; those things that fall outside of our mission are out of bounds and should be ignored.

If an organization puts merit on having an empowered workforce, or if it is required to place a high priority on creativity and innovation, then mission prevents chaos and anarchy. In either situation, mission helps to provide the structure and boundary for people to perform.

This boundary also protects us from attempting to be all things to all people. The business world is undergoing so much change while appearing so dynamic and fluid that it easily takes on assignments that are out of bounds. This willingness to stretch those boundaries leads to confusion and eventually a workforce that has a difficult time distinguishing its purposeful work from its non-valued added work.

Often the more established the organization or the better it appears to be placed in the industry—the greater the temptation. Consider the number of Fortune 1000 companies that have gotten themselves into trouble by trying to be all things or experts in an industry they know little or nothing about. If mergers and acquisitions are a means to accomplish your growth strategy, be conscious of the fact that each organization has its own unique mission. A merger or acquisition forms a new business, with need to re-mission or create an entirely new mission.

3. Mission is a critical element when communicating to your customer. It basically describes what you do, and you gain the benefit of helping your customer to understand what services and products your organization can provide to them. Therefore, mission is both an internal and external tool.

Of equal importance, it informs your customer what you do not do. This helps to establish reasonable expectations and

requests from the customer. Mission helps suppliers and customers to focus.

When a customer understands our mission, he often drives
our creativity. This happens when he has a need that appears to
be within our capability according to our mission. Frequently,
our clients have asked us to create a solution for them, which
on our own, we would not have seen the need or opportunity to
create.

4.   A benefit of mission that is seldom acknowledged is its
       ability to promote teamwork. When people are pursuing
       the same thing, extraordinary things happen. Teams win
       championships, people walk on the moon, a marching
       band creates intricate formations, diseases are cured, and
       prejudice and racism disappear. In general, great things
       happen through ordinary peoples' focus on the task at
       hand—their mission.

5.   The fifth and final benefit I will discuss is perhaps the
       one most directly applicable to the bottom-line. Mission
       is the first criteria for decision making.

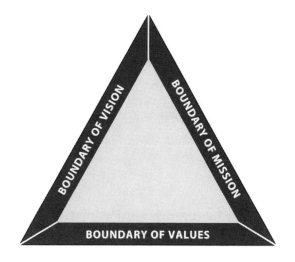

Over the years, I have learned that an organization or executive who has difficulty in making a decision is most often unclear on the mission or has ignored the mission as an evaluation criterion. When a difficult decision arises, the first question should be obvious. *How does this decision affect our mission?* Instead, we hear the typical question. *How does this opportunity affect our bottom-line?*

If the answer is that it enhances or promotes its achievement, then pursue it. Ask some questions. Is it timely? Does it enhance our financial situation? Can we afford it now? If the answer does not support our mission or it hinders its achievement, then drop it immediately. It's out of bounds.

LEADERSHIP ALERT

One of the most impressive examples of mission in action was communicated in the February 25, 1991, issue of *Time* magazine. The article was making a comparison between Wal-Mart and Sears.

"When Sears' 13 directors gathered last week in the spacious, peach-carpeted 68th-floor boardroom, the reports they faced were overwhelmingly bad. A mammoth increase in advertising had scarcely budged sales. Profits were way down. The Christmas selling season was the worst in 15 years. One piece of news especially seemed to mock the setting's regal grandeur. Sears, officially, is no longer America's largest retailer. The new king: Wal-Mart, a onetime backwoods bargain barn that, according to late figures, has pulled past Sears in North American sales . . . Critics say Sears has lost touch with its customers and its mission. As a result, several retail expansions during the past few years have failed . . ."

Leaders beware. If it can happen to a company as strong as Sears, then all companies are certainly vulnerable. (To Sears' credit, their new leadership has made significant strides to return their competitive position; the problem is that it should have never been lost.)

Your mission should be visited every year when conducting the organization's strategic planning session. If necessary, re-mission. In the twenty-four years of De La Porte and Associates, Inc., we have modified our mission three times. In one circumstance, our customers' needs were changing; in another, we decided to pursue a slightly different niche. The third modification was driven by the business climate of the early nineties.

Like the example set by The Perfect Leader, a leader aligned on purpose establishes the model for his organization, which is aligned and unified in order to create competitive advantage.

CHAPTER FOUR

PERFECT LEADER QUALITY #4:
VALUES-BASED
CHARACTER

*"For the time will come when men will not put up with
sound doctrine. Instead, to suit their own desires, they
will gather around them a great number of teachers to say
what their itching ears want to hear. They will turn their
ears away from the truth and turn aside to myths."*

II Timothy 4:3–4

Since 1990 the debate on character has been a political foot-ball. From the time Vice President Dan Quayle challenged the moral value of television character Murphy Brown and received a national backlash, the issue of character has moved to prominence.

The 1992 Presidential election emphasized a strategy of pointing out perceived character flaws. Most were directed at Democratic Candidate Bill Clinton. It polarized the nation and shocked many that the issue of character had so little impact on the voters' final decisions.

Fast-forward to the 1996 Presidential elections. A summer Gallup Poll found that less than 45 percent of the voters trusted (now) President Clinton. On the other hand, Senator Bob Dole, his opponent, scored above 60 percent on the questions evaluating his trust value. The bottom-line was the kick in the stomach.

Sixty-two percent of those polled were voting for Bill Clinton. Trusting or not trusting the President seemed to make little difference to the populace.

Yet the circumstances continue to escalate. The century has turned, but the problem continues to play out. Corporate scandals fill the airwaves with companies like Adelphia and Enron making the headlines on a daily basis. Wall Street stock evaluators come under criticism as they watch stocks fall 80 percent and still have "strong buy" as their continual recommendation.

Have our citizens and country abandoned the very fiber we were built upon—principles and values?

This illustration is not intended to debate the candidates or the business environment. Instead, a far greater question clamors to be answered. What has happened to our country and our concern for the qualities of our leaders? From a time when character was "the issue" for our forefathers until 1996, we have deteriorated to the point that character is no longer a distinguishing issue for our leaders. Can our national problems, which relate to drugs, unwed mothers, fathers shirking their responsibilities, euthanasia, welfare, treatment of the elderly or handicapped, and even our racial prejudices, be linked to something as basic as character? I think the answer is an overwhelming—yes. You must answer the question for yourself.

Does a leader who boasts on MTV, "Of course, I inhaled" bring credibility to our fight against drugs? Does a leader who is referred to as "Slick Willy" and who is under constant investigation for numerous allegations command your desire to follow and carry his message? Character *does* count if we are intent on following the leader's vision, mission, and values.

Is character a requirement of ethical leadership? What kind of character is required? How is it shaped? This chapter will attempt to explore this leadership quality.

The Perfect Leader not only models the true character we need to emulate, but He is very outspoken on what actions and stands we should emphasize.

There are hundreds of Scriptures that describe and show the character of The Perfect Leader. To help us focus, here is a brief introduction.

> 1.   II Timothy 2:14 "Keep reminding them of these things. Warn them before God against quarreling about words; it is of no value, and only ruins those that listen."

Character establishes values on interpersonal health.

> 2.   I Timothy 4:11, 12 "Command and teach these things . . . set an example for the believers with speech, in life, in love, in faith and in purity."

Character walks the talk.

> 3.   I Thessalonians 5:16–18 "Be joyful always; pray continually, give thanks in all circumstances . . ."

Character avoids being discouraged by circumstances.

> 4.   Philippians 4:8 "Finally, brothers, whatever is true, whatever is noble, whatever is right, whatever is pure, whatever is lovely, whatever is admirable—if anything is excellent or praiseworthy—think about such things."

Character focuses on the positive.

> 5.   Philippians 2:4 "Each of you should look not only to your own interest, but also to the interest of others."

Character serves others.

> 6.   Philippians 2:14 "Do everything without complaining or arguing."

Character maintains a cooperative attitude.

> 7.   Ephesians 4:29 "Do not let any unwhole-

some talk come out of your mouths, but only what is helpful for building others up according to their needs, that it may benefit those who listen."

Character catches people doing things right.

8.　Galatians 6:4–5 "Each one should test his own actions. Then he can take pride in himself, without comparing himself to somebody else, for each one should carry his own load."

Character requires self-management.

9.　II Corinthians 4:8,9,16 "We are hard pressed on every side, but not crushed; perplexed . . . but not abandoned; struck down, but not destroyed . . . Therefore, we do not lose heart."

Character demonstrates perseverance.

10.　I Corinthians 15:33 "Do not be misled: "Bad company corrupts good character."

Character protects reputation.

11.　II Corinthians 1:18 [Living Bible] "I am not that type of person. My "yes" means yes."

Character establishes communication that is trusted.

Even though these represent only eleven passages about The Perfect Leader, a clear picture of this man's character is revealed. What's more, these were not empty campaign pledges or promises given by an executive who breaks them the first time a real test comes up. This leader modeled them, giving his followers the opportunity to see character in action. His followers could evaluate, internalize, and apply the lessons themselves. This created the incentive to pass them from generation to generation. While they may not be modeled to the same degree, it is clear what "Perfection" we are to aim for.

No wonder his followers trusted him, believed his words, followed his direction, and were inspired by his day-to-day example. So much so, they continued his vision throughout their entire lifetimes. For most of these followers, their commitments resulted in persecution, hardship, and even death.

THE TWENTY-FIRST-CENTURY LEADERSHIP CRISIS

Let us fast forward to today. Without a doubt, we have a crisis on our hands. The crisis is reflected in the lack of quality, character-based, believable leaders.

Is it a surprise that movements within the United States business community are trying to place leadership emphasis in new and different arenas? Everyone has seen the new emphasis placed on teams. The ultimate team is reportedly the "self-directed team" according to the latest human resource experts and university professors. While teams are not a formal chapter in this book, I can find no example where The Perfect Leader attempted to develop or support the concept of self-directed teams.

Although few business leaders would admit it, a major reason for these new efforts is due to the lack of trust and confidence their employees have in the current "bosses." The workforce has experienced too many broken promises, poor change management, and loss of job security to align genuinely with many of these "bosses." While many leaders are true believers, a change is necessary, and the employee can take much more responsibility. The leaders' own skills are frequently severely lacking in this new work paradigm.

Why all the distrust? This should not be a great mystery to figure out. In the last twenty years, the follower has observed massive lay-offs and the loss of the leader's global position—indictments and special investigators looking into the Presidency, Congress, Wall Street, Fortune 500 Companies, the clergy, and the press to name a few.

When things are predictable and our business patterns are

giving us a reliable history, then managing the business is much simpler. Management can get it done, and few real leaders are necessary. This can be demonstrated by looking at the business trends and responses from 1950 through 1980. Unfortunately or fortunately, we do not operate in *that* world any longer.

We have put our faith in quality circles, total quality management, downsizing, right-sizing, systems thinking, re-engineering, and teams to list a few. Yes, we do have a few measurable successes, but very few of those successes are sustaining. To me, this implies the "trend" was not the true answer, but a mechanism or tool to be used by the persons in charge to get the job done. What was believed to be a long-range commitment turned out, at best, to be a short-term benefit.

The answer all along, during this chaos, was the leader. The followers need a leader who will demonstrate the courage to live his values in front of them, the customers, and the competition. He is a person who is willing to instill a "value-based" system throughout his organization, without compromise. He is a person who is willing to require people to behave and communicate within this system. He is a person who is willing to take the risk and raise the bar of performance and expectation to new world record heights. He is a person who is more concerned with doing what is right than following the out-dated rules, standard operating procedures, and safety nets of the past. Finally, he is a person who is willing to put the money and rewards in place to instill his system.

We have tried to legislate fairness and integrity. EEO, Affirmative Action, diversity training, sexual harassment, etc. have all been put in place to "require" those in charge to do the right things as they relate to their followers. Those seem to be good ideas and nice programs, but they are only marginally successful. Establishing more rules does not change attitudes; it may stop or slow down certain behavior, but it does not help us to know how to act. It leaves a void. It would be like punishing your child for using poor manners, but never teaching him what good manners are or when they should be used.

We only have to check the latest publications of our favorite weekly business magazines to observe the failings of the legislated, rule-based system.

However, when a leader truly values a person, the rules and programs are not necessary to ensure emphasis. The Perfect Leader demonstrated throughout his life the value-based approach. His actions did the talking; his words educated as to his intent. When asked about the greatest command of the New Testament, He responded with two statements. His first response, "Love each other, as I have loved you." What would happen if we could follow that one value? One thing's for sure, we would not have to legislate how to treat or respect another person.

WHAT IS VALUE-BASED LEADERSHIP?

A value-based leader follows two initial steps. First, he selects the key values that he holds near and dear to his own personal being and welfare. Second, he determines the values he wants to see within his workforce when they are interacting with teammates and customers.

To be clear, values for the organization are frequently established by a leadership team. This is appropriate if:

(1) Everyone commits to each value and its implementation.

(2) Everyone believes that when the workforce acts out this value, trust will be enhanced between all parties.

(3) Everyone knows that implementation of these values will create individual empowerment, propelling the organization toward its vision and mission.

Once the values are established, the leader must take responsibility for their definitions, their communications, their implementations, and their sustainability.

In today's business language, these values are frequently referred to as core-guiding principles. The following segments will describe how to establish these values or principles, what must be done to implement them, and how to create sustainability.

QUALITIES OF CORE-GUIDING PRINCIPLES

1.   They must be behaviorally based.

For these principles to be useful, they must have the ability to be seen through a person's actions. Our beliefs and attitudes are usually antecedents to our actions—so they will be reflected as well. As an example, one of our company's principles is, "Do the right thing." An employee must first make a mental decision as to what is right for the circumstance. He must then act in accordance with this decision, uncompromisingly.

2.   They must ensure ethical behavior.

Business is complex at all levels in an organization. The principles will direct individual decisions, moving people's actions toward morally sound as well as legal behavior. In a world with so many gray areas, our principles serve to provide personal and immediate feedback.

Employees must be able to determine with a simple yes or no answer, at the end of the day, if they modeled the principles.

We all lead too many people to provide extensive, daily feedback to each person for each decision and activity he performs. Our principles are the basis for self-management. An individual can provide his own feedback about his total performance when he is clear on what the values are, and he understands their meaning.

The principle must be clear enough that an employee can use it as a decision-making tool.

In our complex and changing world, the reliance on teams or

multiple decision makers compounds the reality of having inconsistent decisions, or perhaps worse, no decisions. Principles, when communicated, explained, and understood, provide a unique set of guidelines to help people respond consistently and accurately. Given their usage in a similar situation, the president of the company and the line employee would essentially make the same decision.

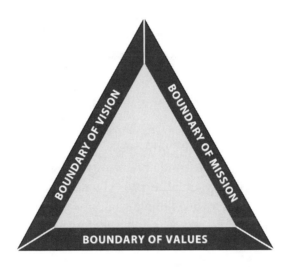

They should provide focus.

Since we can't be all things to all people, our principles help us to prioritize and place emphasis where emphasis is needed. Just as important, they help us to evaluate what is no longer value-added work.

The Perfect Leader gave us many principles to follow. However, two were given as the primary values to drive our attitudes and behaviors. Incidentally, these two values meet all five of the aforementioned criteria.

> Mark 12:30–31 "Love the Lord your God with all your heart and with all your soul and with all your mind and with all your strength." The sec-

ond is this: "Love your neighbor as yourself."
There is no commandment greater than these.

It is no wonder that The Perfect Leader was able to see his vision and mission continue. After his physical presence was no longer needed, his followers simply had to be vision driven, aligned on purpose, and demonstrate value-based character—all of which had been established and modeled before their very eyes on a daily basis for three years.

He had effectively and efficiently provided a message and framework that would sustain to the end of mankind. That is perfect leadership.

IMPLEMENTING THE CORE-GUIDING PRINCIPLES

1.   Link the principles to the Vision and Mission Statement.

A set of principles to guide behavior will have little meaning if they are not instrumental in providing action. What kind of action is needed? Pure and simple, action results in achievement of our mission while providing momentum toward our vision. Anything else would have to be seriously questioned as a non-essential or non-value-added activity.

Leaders *must* help connect these three elements every chance they get. People do not easily make the connection on their own, so leaders must consciously bridge an action to present successes and the future.

A basketball coach will help his players see clearly the linkage between conditioning, practice habits, and the achievement of the team's goals, mission, and vision. Successful coaches instill the values needed to compete in the game well before the game starts. In practice, off-season conditioning, discipline in the classroom, and accountability of their own personal behavior are a few areas where the game is won. Mental toughness is a value not a goal.

2.   Document and communicate each principle's meaning.

Warren Bennis, in his book *Leaders,* states " . . . leaders must provide meaning."[3] How true. No one wants to be measured against a standard that is unknown to us or unclear. People need to understand the definition and interpretation attached to each principle.

Each principle should have a brief and pointed explanation as to its meaning. You may reference the appendix to get an example of how we handle this information at De La Porte & Associates, Inc. It is often a good strategy to allow the followers to have an active part in defining the values as well as determining how to implement them.

Leadership should not only provide this in writing, but take personal responsibility for the orientation of the workforce. This means getting up in front of the employees and explaining what they mean to them. Fielding questions and filling in the implied meaning is critical. This should never be delegated to a lieutenant at the front end. The Perfect Leader clearly took this responsibility Himself; no one else could provide the passion and clarity of meaning.

A common mistake (I have seen with my clients) is putting a lot of energy into the creation and initial orientation of the principles, and then getting too busy in day-to-day responsibilities to follow through. It is believed that this up-front energy and emphasis will carry the initiative to fruition. (More likely, they put many other activities ahead of this culture-shaping and time-intensive exercise.)

Hanging a vision statement on the wall for all to see is not communication; it is artwork. It will command no more attention than your best oil paintings.

3.   Link the principles to your performance appraisal.

We get what we measure and reward. If you are frustrated by a lack of visible evidence that your efforts to establish vision, mission, and principles are making little difference, then examine three areas.

First, are we modeling our principles for everyone to learn and buy into their credibility? Second, are we measuring peoples' performance and attitudes through our principles? Third, are we rewarding the desired behaviors and punishing the undesired behaviors?

I firmly believe that the only performance appraisal necessary is one built directly on your principles, with a section that places emphasis on vision and mission. Any job or function can be easily connected through performance to the core-guiding principles.

People soon learn to do what they are rewarded to do. They are smart enough to know what really counts and what is rhetoric.

As a 22-two-year-old high school teacher, I observed a situation that has remained with me throughout my career. This lifelong learning event centered on rewarding the wrong behavior and punishing the desired behavior.

The policy in our school district, at the time, was to provide one day of sick leave for each month of our contract. Most teachers were paid for nine months so they earned nine sick days. If the time was not used, it could be accumulated from one year to the next. The intent was perfectly honest. Provide a safety net for a good teacher who was ill and protect his salary. However, if you left the district or retired, you lost any accumulated sick days with no compensation.

A teacher I will call Joe decided to retire early. He had been with the district nearly twenty-five years and had accumulated over 180 sick days. He had been a good and reliable employee, did his job, and came to work faithfully. To make a long story short, the teaching year consisted of 183 days. Joe showed up the first day of the year and called in sick the remaining 182! He not only was rewarded for doing the undesired behavior (staying home), but he had been punished for doing the desired behavior (getting no reward for his good attendance while anyone calling in sick still got paid). This example is not to debate ethics, but it is intended to illustrate that people tend to do what rewards them.

4.   Use every opportunity to review principles and to remind people how principles manifest themselves into the everyday life of the organization.

In the Old Testament, the Jewish people were taught how to transmit their values into the hearts and minds of their children.

> Deuteronomy 6:6–9 "These commandments that I give you today are to be upon your hearts. Impress them on your children. Talk about them when you sit at home and when you walk along the road, when you lie down and when you get up. Tie them as symbols on your hands and bind them on your foreheads. Write them on the door-frames of your houses and on your gates."

Allow me to take some personal liberty with this text and translate it into leadership language for the twenty-first century.

"Leaders, take every opportunity you have to emphasize the values you want your followers to adhere to and believe in. Use every public forum, every staff meeting, every publication, and every means of communication to emphasize the importance of these values and to see what it looks like when we demonstrate the desired actions. If you don't make it your job and priority, don't expect results. Take the message of internalizing the values seriously. Do not delegate this responsibility."

SUSTAINING OUR CORE-GUIDING PRINCIPLES

The greatest challenge to leadership, regarding the principles, is not in their selection, in their formation, or in their communication. The real challenge is in *sustaining* them as a cultural boundary.

Like so many "new and hot" ideas or initiatives, there is much focus placed on the principles in the early stages. At first, everyone is excited to describe their good work. The tendency then is to relax and watch how this high-level approach to leadership will transform our culture on its own. Good intent, poor delivery. At this point, the "words on the walls" settle into oblivion, just like so many other initiatives that failed to work after their coronation. No wonder the employee refers to this as the "flavor of the month"!

It takes persistence and constant attention in order to instill the principles into the daily interactions of the people.

I attended the University of New Mexico on a basketball scholarship. My coach, Bob King, started every practice with the fundamentals I learned as a seven-year-old: dribbling, shooting, right and left hand lay-ups, passing, and foot movements for defense. I must have shot a million lay-ups in my career. Much has been forgotten from those days, but the fundamentals are still sustained. Why? They were too important to our overall success not to be emphasized every day. Is it surprising that Coach King has the basketball court named in his honor at the famous "Pit," or that he is in the New Mexico Hall of Fame? Not to his players.

It takes persistence and constant attention in order to instill the principles into the daily interactions of people. If you are thinking, "I just read that a few sentences ago," you are correct. I learned from The Perfect Leader that if the message is critical, repeat it frequently. The Perfect Leader must think being joyful and rejoicing are important because he tells us more than seventy times in the New Testament to "be joyful and rejoice."

We will always have to put an emphasis on how the principles and values are communicated. However, once they are the norm (the way the organization acts routinely and unconsciously), then we can take a reinforcing approach versus an establishing approach. At this point, the people within the organization will protect the principle.

Remember the Scripture that explained how the Jewish people implanted their values on their children? This is a perfect example of how a nation of people has continued to survive and prosper through decades of trials and tribulations.

When the principles have become the norm, a cultural transformation has taken place—planned, directed, and shaped by the leader.

Here are a few ideas to help this transformation along.

1.   Use the principles as step one in the new employee selection process.

When a person applies for employment at our company (and we are in a legitimate search mode), we give him a copy of our vision, mission, and values. He is asked to review them overnight and to let us know if he believes he can support and work within this framework. We have received many compliments about this approach. More importantly, about 25 percent of the applicants decide not to pursue the opportunity. I respect their reasoning and know that this process saved both of us many missed expectations down the road.

2.   Explain major decisions to the workforce within the context of the core-guiding principles.

A leader must link the principles to critical decisions. If we are to be developers of our workforce, they need to observe how the process of using vision, mission, and values as a decision triangle actually works.

A few years ago two companies merged. By doing so, they

increased their capability of competing and surviving in a rapidly changing industry. My client's firm had adopted the vision "to win the aerospace race," as well as a set of values that was to protect the people and productivity of their plant. While the anxiety of the merger still created much concern, the leader effectively used the vision and values of the organization to demonstrate how the decision modeled the values and helped the employees win the "aerospace race." Jobs were protected, and the business was more competitive. As for the leader, he has continued to grow. Today, Bob Coutts is in charge of an $8 billion business group with one of the nation's largest aerospace companies.

3. Promote and reward the people that perform *AND* model the principles.

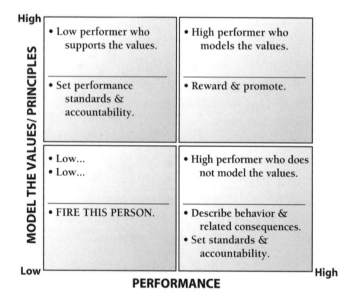

4. Be willing to make the tough decisions.

Just as important as rewarding and promoting people for modeling the principles and being high performers, the flip side must also happen. Non-performers of the values or work must be dealt with quickly and firmly.

When working with clients, I always ask the leader how committed he is to the principles. Then I test him; I ask a question he must answer.

If your best engineer refuses to follow the philosophies and actions required by your values, will you compromise your stand (make an exception) or fire him?

A case in point, what did the Chicago Bulls' decisions on the handling of Dennis Rodman tell you about its leadership and its commitment to the team's values?

A case in point, what did Major League Baseball convey to its players and umpires concerning the handling of the Roberto Alomar spitting situation?

Cases in point, pick up a *Business Week, Time,* or *Fortune,* and interpret the messages clearly delivered by leaders' actions. What is really important to them?

5. Make the Big Three the primary framework for all decision making. Vision, mission, and values are the decision triangle.

The answer to the following questions will assure the decision is in alignment with your organization's culture.
   a. Does "it" move us toward our vision?
   b. Is "it" within our purpose (mission)?
   c. Does "it" violate any of our core-guiding principles?

6. Teach the process to everyone in the organization.

While the leader may be the catalyst, it is imperative that all participants understand the process. The process will focus on why the principles were created, how they were developed, what they are supposed to accomplish, how to live by them, and finally how to implement and sustain them.

One of the best jobs I have observed in using these six steps to implement and shape a business is Toledo, Ohio, based Libbey Glass Company. From their CEO, to their senior staff, to their managers, to their frontline supervisors, they have conducted personal presentations, roundtables, breakfast meetings, linked their performance system, formalized publications, and changed everyone's computer screen saver to reflect their commitment and message. This is truly an organization that understands and demonstrates leadership through its vision, mission, and values.

CHANGING THE GAME OLD VS. NEW TESTAMENT

The Perfect Leader as always gives us a clear picture of where today's leaders should place their attention.

If we were to focus on the Old Testament, we would see that the people were given rule after rule to follow. As we can see from Scripture, the only real consistency was how quickly and skillfully the rules were broken, modified, or ignored.

While the Ten Commandments are sent directly from God, mankind has failed to follow them. Rules seem to be fine to limit people, but they are not very fulfilling to obey. Eventually, rules become a challenge to break, or people become apathetic about them. They tend to tell us what we should not do, but they seldom tell us what to do. There were even groups that thought the rules were not complete enough, so they added their own set. In time, the society was bound by legalistic limitations. In business, we would refer to this as bureaucracy.

In fact, rules tend to make us feel like we are being pushed. Therefore, there is a tendency to do the minimum expected. On the other hand, values create a feeling of being pulled forward and allow the energy within us to expand our performance.

It is no different today. People are frequently interested in only supporting the rules that affect or benefit them directly. Without constant policing, the rules will be broken.

You may think this is nonsense. Well, go back to 1996 and a speed limit of 55 mph. Remember 80 percent of the cars passing 20 percent of the cars that were going 55 mph? Not only were they passed, the person doing the passing was frequently put out by the "slow traffic." Now if the state police were present, we all slowed down and obeyed the law until they left.

Leaders were basically the cops. As a result of this rules-based environment, we helped to create an adversarial relationship with the employee. It demanded that the person in charge watch to see who was breaking the rules as opposed to who was keeping them. You were punished for breaking the rules, but you were seldom rewarded for keeping them. There is no fulfillment for the individual employee in this system.

Try this comparison to our business culture.

Old Testament Observations	"Old" Business Methods
God, the boss, is viewed as only a dispenser of pain and punishment.	Bosses distrusted, viewed as only protecting corporate and upper management interests.
The emphasis appeared to focus on catching someone doing something wrong.	Focuses on finding problems, therefore, nearly all feedback is catching someone doing something wrong.
The methodology to follow was to know and obey the rules.	Virtually no difference, except not everybody knew the implied rules.
Only the high priest had the ability to enforce rules and consequences.	Only management had the ability to enforce rules and consequences.
There were few leaders, usually one at a time.	Well-defined hierarchies with less and less power as you move down.
Many died for the cause on both sides.	Turnover, dissatisfaction, downsizing, lost customers; virtually no difference.
Frequent rebellions.	Unions, apathy, loss of productivity, leaving a company to go work for a competitor.

Please do not misinterpret this message. Rules are necessary to support principles, and they help to provide some order and structure. However, the volumes of rules that have become our albatross today serve mostly to slow our ability to change and respond to our customers and employees. They also are easier to manage, allowing many "bosses" the excuse they need to remain in the twentieth century, mostly because of the black and white nature of rules.

Is it any surprise that we are all sick of filling out volumes of forms that require signatures in triplicate? I signed eight papers the last time I bought a car—I paid for it in cash!

The Perfect Leader gives us very few rules in the New Testament. Instead, he gives us many principles and challenges the way we think, act, and speak. He encourages us to love one another in all things we do—yes, even business—and to lead by serving those that follow us.

The results of this approach will create a very different matrix. If we were to examine the method and benefit, it will become apparent that it was not Tom Peters, Peter Senge, or any other twentieth-century guru who first spoke and modeled this leadership approach. It was, in fact, The Perfect Leader.

Perfect Leader, New Testament	Benefits to Business
Lead through principles not rules.	Transfers ownership to all levels of the organization and requires more self-management and accountability.
When dealing with people, encourage, praise when due, find the positive they contribute.	People feel valued, worthy, and appreciated . . . therefore putting their energy into the work.
Teach others to do the job, and then let them do the job.	Empowered and confident people, constantly developing.
Keep the message simple, and repeat it often.	Clear understanding, and therefore, higher commitment.
Challenge people to get involved, think, and act.	Clear understanding, and therefore, higher commitment.

HOW MANY PRINCIPLES SHOULD WE HAVE?

There is no magic answer or number. However, I believe they should be brief, easy to recall, and have a deep personal *revelation* to the leader. (Ultimately, this *revelation* should be felt by the followers as well.)

While people do not have to memorize the principles like they should the Vision and Mission Statements, a quick reference card should be readily available. If people are not intimately familiar with them, it will be nearly impossible to demonstrate the principles. It will also be difficult to create accountability in order to model and share them.

I expect our employees to carry our vision, mission, and values in their day-timer system or palm pilots. We provide a laminated card and expect it to be reviewed frequently. If each employee applies these factors to his daily activities, then the employee is free to act within this boundary. This is a true basis for empowerment. These values/principles serve to guide them in "how to act."

It has been my approach to recommend to our clients to formulate no more than ten principles. My rationale is simple. God gave us Ten Commandments; so ten principles seem within reason. Regardless of the number selected, each must be important enough for the leader to provide unconditional support.

How intensely did The Perfect Leader feel about his teaching?

> Philippians 4:9 "Whatever you have learned or received or heard from me, or seen in me–put it into practice. And the God of peace will be with you."

CHAPTER FIVE

PERFECT LEADER QUALITY #5:
SERVICE NOT SERVITUDE

" . . . You know that in this world kings are tyrants and
officials lord over the people beneath them. But
among you it should be quite different. Whoever wants
to be a leader among you must be your servant, and
whoever wants to be first must become your slave. For even
I, the Son of Man, came here not to be served but to serve
others, and to give you my life as a ransom for many.

Matthew 20:25–28 [New Living Translation]

Today we frequently hear the need to change our paradigm about how we lead. A paradigm is a set of standards, beliefs, and attitudes that creates the boundary in which we think and act. Our paradigm dictates the policies, procedures, and methodologies we create. Most significantly, it provides the basis for our viewpoints.

Paradigms affect the way we look at leadership and management. Therefore, they help to determine our actions toward our customers, teammates, competitors, and employees. As long as we operate within our paradigm, it seems right to us and is very likely supported by our organizational norms.

Paradigms create filters so we can quickly discern what seems right to us. We all have paradigms, some helpful and some harmful, some accurate and some inaccurate. In any case, they shape our ability to lead. They serve as filters by letting some information into our thinking and preventing other information from penetrating our thought process.

Some of you will debate this next statement. However, the evidence overwhelmingly supports it. We generally hire people to serve our needs, and our pursuit up the corporate ladder is often about having more power.

The Perfect Leader challenges the old management paradigm. He states that even the "minor" official or first-line supervisor lords it over those "beneath" him. I do not think he was referring to only the position of the official but also his attitude. This type of activity helps to establish a paradigm that puts the leaders on one plateau and the followers on a lower level, separated by a chasm of trust and privilege.

One simple example should validate that our talk is often not the walk when it comes to serving our followers and customers. When our profits are lower than the board of directors were expecting and they choose to downsize, is there equal concern for the lower-level employees? Do they get the out-placement services, golden parachutes, buy-outs, etc.?

My purpose in this discussion is not to criticize whether these programs are right or wrong, but to validate that this "paradigm" is not one of a servant-leader. This example should point out how valid our paradigms are for predicting behavior.

The change in the world market place and our position in this global competition require leaders to examine their current method of operation. For many, the observation should result in the creation of a new leadership paradigm—

one I believe that has been there for thousands of years—the leadership paradigm of The Perfect Leader (to serve those He leads).

In June 1993, the cover story in *Training* magazine, written by Chris Lee and Ron Zemke, was entitled *The Search for Spirit in the Workplace.* The article looked at the recent talk about visions, values, and purposes in corporate America. While it was a very good article, what caught my attention was the section that looked at the servant-leader. The article stated, "Most credit Robert K. Greenleaf, one-time management researcher at AT&T and lifelong philosopher, with introducing the idea in a 1970 essay called *The Servant as Leader.*"

While the essay excerpts were interesting, The Perfect Leader had introduced this approach to leadership some two thousand years earlier—not as a philosophy—but as a real life, working model.

One other motivator begs us to examine this leadership style. It facilitates the current initiatives and trends that we are driving in corporate America to return us to competitive advantage.

If you are serious about being the best leader you can be, then answer the questions on this simple test. Check which leadership approach would best support the statements below.

Servant-leader or Traditional Leader

1. Push decision making to the lowest competence level in the organization. _____ or ____
2. Empower the workforce. _____ or _____
3. Build trust. _____ or _____
4. Market-driven product focus. _____ or _____
5. Develop teams and teamwork. _____ or _____
6. Promote diversity. _____ or _____
7. Promote innovation & creativity. _____ or _____
8. Coach and counsel employees. _____ or _____
9. Consultative selling. _____ or _____
10. Outrageous customer service. _____ or _____

If the above quiz did not challenge you to examine The Perfect Leader's servant-leader style, then your paradigm is working overtime. There is no question; we cannot effectively implement the ten behaviors above with a traditional approach.

BELIEFS, ATTITUDES, AND STANDARDS

If this truly is a paradigm in need of changing, and paradigms are made up of beliefs, attitudes, and standards, then perhaps the examination should begin here.

Webster's defines belief as: (1) a conviction that certain things are true, (2) trust and confidence in, (3) acceptance of, (4) an opinion; expectation.

Attitude is defined as: (1) a bodily posture meant to show a mental state, emotion, or mood (2) a manner of acting, feeling, or thinking that shows one's opinion.

Finally, standard is defined as: (1) something established for use as a rule or basis for comparison or judging capacity, quantity, content, value, extent, quality, etc.

The first point to make regarding the definitions is that it is easy to see how our beliefs and attitudes establish our standards. Once in place, the three areas create the filters that in time become our paradigms. The paradigms approve of the way we lead and act within them. We don't even question our motives or actions.

Because this is a book dedicated to the topic of leadership, the beliefs I will examine are only four in number. However, these four help to form a solid foundation for others to build upon. It is likely that every leader must grapple with at least one of these beliefs. It is also likely that no leader has more than two of these as primary beliefs.

Dysfunctional Belief #1: I must have control.

There is probably not a leader or manager today that does not want to have some control over the work and the people doing the work. The operational word is "some."

The person who is always driven to be in control or who is seeking to be in control of others is modeling this belief.

Given this belief, what attitudes do you imagine this person to possess? With these beliefs and attitudes, can you predict the standards he would create? The filter is now in place.

Unfortunately, this person frequently gains a reputation as being dictatorial, uncaring, impersonal, lacking empathy, and stifling others willingness and ability to perform and think.

Enter The Perfect Leader's challenge to be a servant to those you lead. Can't you just imagine the internal debates going on in this person's head? That is, if the message gets through the filter at all.

To allow someone other than myself to be in control puts me at risk and out of control. Can you hear the struggle?

We only have to remember Watergate and observe the destructive decisions rendered by President Nixon to witness the impacts to his staff, family, and nation by his relentless quest to have ultimate control.

Dysfunctional Belief #2: I must be the expert.

While the first belief leads to a competitiveness that emphasizes winning, this belief creates a person who believes he is always right.

This "know-it-all" attitude of superiority translates to his followers that their opinion doesn't really count. The inflexible communication tends to turn people off, and it creates a feeling of disinterest in talking to this person.

It is difficult for this person to admit that he is wrong and to apologize. The real tragedy shows up when this person lacks the personal relationships to fulfill his life. He is often described as arrogant, condescending, and patronizing.

How does this person translate The Perfect Leader's message—to serve those you lead? He must be willing to allow others to have more say and input. The guarantee of rightness is at risk.

Dysfunctional Belief #3: I must have harmony.

At the onset, this belief might appear to be no problem. After all, doesn't everyone want world peace and a work and family environment that are free of problems?

That's the problem; there are problems everywhere! We do

not live in a perfect world . . . yet. This belief has a very damaging outcome for those who practice within its framework.

The first problem is one that this leader too often abdicates, for fear of appearing uncooperative or uncaring of others opinions and priorities. He appears too complacent.

The second problem stems from the first. Decision making can come to a standstill waiting for everyone to agree and reach consensus. Confrontation is always seen as destructive, and conflict goes underground.

Finally, the mode of operation too often becomes passive manipulation. Since this person is generally cooperative, it can create a sense of guilt if the person does not demonstrate the same degree in return. Hurt feelings and an unwillingness to deal with confrontation occur frequently.

To be a servant-leader, one must demonstrate courage and risk taking. For too many, this type of leadership appears weak and passive, while many others will have difficulty with the over emphasis on risk and conflict aversion.

Dysfunctional Belief #4: I must be recognized.

We all have worked for the person who seems to garnish all the credit, whether he did all the work or not. This belief leads a person to the all too frequent use of the word "I."

Since recognition and popularity easily go hand in hand, this leader could have a tendency to appear interested only in his own well-being and agenda. When this is true, people may find this person's communications to be oriented to what he wants to hear or to be political in nature. His verbal skills can lead to manipulation in order to fulfill his needs.

While this person frequently possesses the charm, wit, and ability to communicate, the underlying belief can create a message that is difficult to trust.

Clearly, this belief can eliminate the message from The Perfect Leader; the leader must serve those he leads. After all, the servant-leader may not be recognized at all, except by his followers.

The impeachment hearings of then President Clinton, in the United States Congress, brought to light a very real problem of recognition. Those close to President Clinton have indicated his ultimate wish to go down in history as a great President. (Is it possible that this need of recognition has impaired his judgment? Did this cloud decisions as to what is in the best interest of our nation or even speak about the on-going embarrassment his actions have caused his family?) More evidence of this problem may have appeared during the Enduring Freedom War in Iraq. The unspoken code that past presidents do not publicly criticize current presidents was broken. If not for recognition, why was this done? Others certainly were providing the same criticism.

DO I REALLY VALUE THOSE WHO FOLLOW?

I have noticed when my parents, teachers, coaches, or any other people in my life have an important message to get across, they repeat it frequently.

The Perfect Leader must have thought the message about being a servant-leader, providing service, or just valuing a servant attitude was important. I have found over ninety Scriptures that address the topic in one form or another.

At the fundamental root of this "servant-leader" approach is a belief, an attitude, and a standard. The Perfect Leader summed it up for us in I Peter 4:8–10.

> "Above all, love each other deeply, because love covers over a multitude of sins. Offer hospitality to one another without grumbling. Each one should use whatever gift he has received to serve others, . . ."

While I may be different from you, there are requirements I set in place before I render service to someone.

* Do I believe this person has earned my service?
* Is this person important enough for me to serve?

- ◆ Does this person want or need my service?
- ◆ Is it worth my investment?
- ◆ Is it required by my values?

(So on and so forth.) I have tried to determine if this person is someone I truly value and therefore worthy of my service. While The Perfect Leader would likely handle this completely different, my point is made. For me, to be willing to serve I must value the person. It would be much easier if it were a family member or close friend that I loved, but the entry fee to the "servant-leader" game is being valued.

My motives are not as pure and as unselfish as they should be. I am not even in The Perfect Leader's zip code. However, I recall a very important quote that seems to fit nicely into this win-win approach. In his book, *See You at the Top,* Zig Ziglar states, "You can have everything in life you want, if you will just help enough other people get what they want."[4]

While The Perfect Leader was unselfish and did not possess our weaknesses for the four dysfunctional beliefs, (win at all cost, must be right, must be accepted, and must gain recognition), He still had a vision and mission to accomplish. The servant-leader approach obviously served his purpose. It aligned with his vision, mission, and values, and it got results. More importantly for his followers, it attuned them with his role as their leader.

How could they not want to follow a leader who met their needs first?

There we have it. The belief—people are of value. The attitude—serve others needs first. The standard—we know the approach works when others want to follow. This paradigm effectively filtered out the dysfunctional behaviors mentioned earlier in this chapter. It also assured that the followers would be aligned with the vision and values.

CHARACTERISTICS OF THE SERVANT-LEADER

There are many characteristics that could be discussed in the arena of leadership. Actually, several have been introduced in the earlier chapters.

There are three that deserve an entire chapter. They are the role of The Perfect Leader as a *developer* of his followers, the demonstration of uncompromising *courage,* and the emphasis this leader puts on *encouragement.*

Many other characteristics make the servant-leader model a unique and leading edge approach for the twenty-first century. A couple of these demand some thought and examples from The Perfect Leader.

- Inspiring trust
- Forgiveness

The servant-leader inspires trust with his followers.

Obviously, we do not follow people through challenging and difficult situations if we do not trust them. So what must they demonstrate for us to trust them?

Wilson Learning Corporation, in Edina, Minnesota, has addressed this issue in a way that has helped thousands of my clients. I believe it is very applicable to The Perfect Leader's example.

To inspire trust, a person must demonstrate and communicate six elements of his person.

1. One must demonstrate a sense of propriety, which is the ability to meet a person's expectations. We may often think this has only to do with appearance, demeanor, and protocol; however, it includes the expectations of a person's entire behavior. How do I expect "my leader" to treat me and represent me with his actions?

2. The trusted person must demonstrate his competence. In

other words, he must be good at his given profession. The operative word is demonstrate.

3. A highly trusted person conveys and follows through with positive intent. To use an old axiom, he truly works to create a win-win atmosphere and outcome.

4. We tend to trust someone with whom we have something in common. Commonality gives the impression that this person must be okay because he is similar in some way to me.

5. A trusted person is one that is credible to us. He is a person who walks his talk, follows through, behaves ethically, and keeps his word and commitments.

6. Finally, to have trust in a person, we must believe he can see the world from our point of view. In other words, he must possess empathy.

With this research from Wilson Learning as a backdrop, we can observe what Scripture reveals to us about The Perfect Leader. Did He demonstrate propriety? Was He competent? Did He establish positive intent? Did He establish a level of commonality? Was He credible? Was He empathetic?

Let us first examine the area of **propriety.** The driving issue? To what degree did He meet the expectations of his followers?

The best way to answer the question is by first trying to figure out what his followers expected. We know from historical research that his followers (disciples) were young and worked in professions other than what He was asking them to do.

Therefore, we can assume that basic expectations included things like teaching them what they needed to know, allowing them to make mistakes, being available for coaching and counseling, being clear with communication, and being patient and understanding.

I won't take the time to elaborate on each of these areas, but the following are just a few of the Scriptures that validate how effectively He met their expectations.

Matthew 10:1–42   Matthew 28:16–20
Matthew 17:19–20   Mark 3:13–16
Mark 6:7–13   Mark 6:45–52

The next test demonstrates the degree to which The Perfect Leader exhibited his **competence.** Since we established in chapter four that his purpose was to teach and preach, then we should determine if the Scriptures record his competency.

Mark 6:50–52   Mark 6:1–6
Mark 1:38–39   Mark 6:32–34
Luke 11:1–4   Luke 12:22–34

The third challenge on the path to inspiring trust is the element of conveying **positive intent.** Was The Perfect Leader concerned about a positive outcome for his followers? Again, we can turn to the Scriptures for this revelation.

> Luke 6:27–28, 31 "But I tell you who hear me: Love your enemies, do good to those who hate you, bless those who curse you, pray for those that mistreat you. . . . Do to others as you would have them do to you."

In order to gain a high level of trust, the follower must believe that there is a degree or element of **commonality** between him and the leader. Since each person is different, this can become a significant challenge. The following examples demonstrate how well The Perfect Leader met his followers' needs in this area.

Scripture records that The Perfect Leader was born to common parents; He was a carpenter from Nazareth, attended to his friends, and interacted with all social levels and stations of humanity. These were common characteristics with many of his followers.

Finally, and perhaps most importantly, to be trusted, The

Perfect Leader must establish Himself as a **credible** person. The following Scriptures help to validate this factor.

John 5:24	John 20:30–31
John 13:34	Luke 24:13–49
John 14:6	

Empathy is demonstrated by the conscious need to demonstrate the five characteristics to his followers.

The Perfect Leader's ability and willingness to set an example personally in order to inspire trust is a powerful demonstration of his desire to serve others versus having others serve Him.

While a chapter is dedicated to discussing forgiveness, it is critical to include a brief link here to being a servant-leader.

The servant-leader is forgiving.

The most difficult characteristic the servant-leader exhibits is the willingness to forgive. Please notice the word is willingness and not ability. Willingness implies that this is something all of us can do; it is not a skill. Then what is the problem? We often just do not want to forgive. It may not serve our selfish purpose or motivation. In addition, the un-forgiven have likely not earned forgiveness.

This puts a very different light on the subject. I am in control of this decision. Yes, it is a decision; so if forgiveness is not granted, the choice and outcome was solely mine. No one else is to blame. No other circumstance is going to be sufficient for hanging blame either; it is and was my choice.

Leadership is not easy; being a servant-leader is even more difficult. However, if we are not honest with ourselves first, we have no chance. Many people have hurt us, just screwed up royally, displayed dishonest behavior, stabbed us in the back, or . . .

Traditional management paradigms would tell us to ignore or punish the people who have wronged us. While the person may still need to be fired, we can forgive. After all, which of us has never made a critical mistake or delivered an insult? Thank goodness some of my former bosses forgave me.

The following Scriptures support The Perfect Leader's teaching on forgiveness.

Luke 23:34   Mark 11:25   Colossians 3:13

To me the most haunting challenge in Scripture that relates to leadership is found in Luke 12:48.

> " . . . From everyone who has been given much, much will be demanded; and from the one who has been entrusted with much, much more will be asked."

I have been given many skills and talents. I have been entrusted with the careers and livelihoods of my associates. I have been entrusted with the confidences and revenues of my clients. I have health, wealth, and a great family. Is asking me to be a servant-leader too much? Absolutely not!

CHAPTER SIX

PERFECT LEADER QUALITY #6:
DEMONSTRATE UNCOMPROMISING COURAGE

"He plied him with many questions,
but Jesus gave him no answer."
Luke 23:9

"When he was accused by the chief priests and the
elders, he gave no answer. Then Pilate asked him,
"Don't you hear the testimony they are bringing against you?"
But Jesus made no reply, not even to a single charge—
to the great amazement of the governor."

Matthew 27:12–14

There are many examples, as we will explore later, of The Perfect Leader demonstrating courage during his life and leadership. None, however, strikes me as so incredible as the situation referenced in the above Scripture.

What courage it must have taken, knowing you were innocent of the charges leveled at you. Yet to fulfill the purpose in which He was sent to complete, it required Him to offer no defense on his own behalf. His silence was deafening.

The assault came not only in lies and insults, but it came

in physical and psychological abuse. In front of his followers, friends, and family, He was cast as a common criminal with no one to stand beside him or even offer a defense.

It is one thing to be silent when we are guilty, but this is unheard of during an accusation we know to be false. For those of us who have received a speeding ticket, we probably were long overdue for one. Think how easy it was to try to defend your actions. Think, when you may have truly been innocent of the ticket, what actions did you take? Even in a losing battle, the chance to have our say at least made the "unfair action" a little easier to tolerate.

So what leadership quality does this example teach us, and how does it apply to our everyday pursuit of being a quality leader?

Courage is a relative characteristic and must be examined in light of the context and framework of the situation. *Courage is only courageous when personal risk or reputation is at stake.* One other factor is required for there to be demonstrated courage; there must be viable alternatives from which to choose. If there are no choices, then I maintain it is not truly courage— maybe bravery, but not courage.

COURAGE AND RISK

In our society, being a "risk taker" is a highly sought after characteristic. To the point, at times, the person who is labeled as "too cautious or risk avoider" is often seen as lacking in the qualities required to be a leader. He is perceived to be too weak.

The Perfect Leader gives us a frequent reminder of the relationship between courage and risk.

> Joshua 1:9 "Have I not commanded you? Be strong and courageous. Do not be terrified; do not be discouraged, for the Lord your God will be with you wherever you go."

I interpret the first section of the quote, "Have I not commanded you?" to remind us that we all have a charge and a role to fulfill within the responsibility of our assigned function. This charge could have been the expectations of a board of directors, a boss, a customer, our family, or a stakeholder. *Someone is expecting us to act when necessary.* This charge forms a basis for our accountability.

The action to be taken will not be an easy decision, and now it will likely put us or our people and organization at risk. The Perfect Leader has warned us that we must display strength.

What could require us to demonstrate strength? It could constitute any number of possibilities. The action may not be popular; it could require a change from the comfortable way of doing things. It could expose us to severe consequences, or it may challenge management. It could cause more effort and work from the employees; it could risk the company's future or our financial situation. Whatever the situation, it will take strength and conviction. In our mind's eye, the potential of personal impact is exposed.

The Perfect Leader knew that many so-called leaders lack the strength to be courageous.

His next observation is significant to understanding courage.

"Do not be terrified." Not one of us is immune to fear. We all have something that can paralyze our thoughts, decisions, and actions. Terror is an extreme response to fear. What may appear to us as an easy decision or course of action, as we observe another's behavior, may be terrifying to them. The reason is simple. If we are that relaxed with the required action, it must not require courage or strength on our part to execute. For example, one person may find that speaking in front of a thousand people is "no sweat." However, for another person, it is terrifying and requires both courage and strength.

While being terrified is in the present, "Do not be discouraged" talks of the effect over time. Obviously, the actions and decisions we make will be played out over time. It often takes more courage and strength when the impact of our actions will not be readily visible. The weariness of this type of situation can cause us to worry and become anxious. The result is discouragement.

> In Philippians 4:6–7, "Do not be anxious about anything, but in everything, by prayer and petition, with thanksgiving, present your request to God. And the peace of God, which transcends all understanding, will guard your hearts and your minds in Christ Jesus."

Matthew 6:25–34 devotes an incredibly insightful passage to the follies of worry. It concludes with some powerful advice.

> Matthew 6:34 "Therefore do not worry about tomorrow, for tomorrow will worry about itself. Each day has enough trouble of its own."

Finally, The Perfect Leader tells Joshua that He will be with him where ever he goes. Support from someone is a critical factor in being courageous. A kind word, a word of praise, and an acknowledgement that our action is appreciated—all of these may be the ingredients that give us the strength to move forward. Even courageous and strong leaders need someone to support them.

COURAGE AND ETHICS

For some leaders, it would be easy to demonstrate courage if there were no check and balance system.

Ethics serve as a check and balance for the leader's courage. The dynamic that is created is much like taking a rubber band with one loop placed around the right index finger and the other loop placed around the left index finger. As you spread your hands apart, the properties of the rubber band come into play. This creates a tension on both index fingers.

Ethics serves as the "rubber band" for courage. Without the

pressure created by ethics, courage could become reckless and irresponsible. A case in point would be Adolph Hitler.

Few could argue that he did not lead or show courage. However, his lack of moral ethics not only doomed his leadership, but it also created extreme hardships for the people he was charged to lead.

I suggest that there are far too many examples in American business and government where a person's courage far out weighed his ethics, resulting in disaster. A lack of the courage necessary to adhere to moral behavior leads to ethical wrongs. Remember the Enron situation.

We live in a universe based on order. The Perfect Leader challenges us to be courageous and strong, but to carry out this action with the balance of the other leadership characteristics described in this book. Order, not recklessness or selfish ambition, is the approach that delivers the result.

The Perfect Leader recognized this concern whenever a person was given power. In Joshua 1:8, just prior to his charge to Joshua, the "ethics" of leadership were put into context.

> "Do not let this Book of the Law depart from your mouth; meditate on it day and night, so that you may be careful to do everything written in it. Then you will be prosperous and successful."

COURAGE AND DOING THE RIGHT THING

There are many times that doing the right thing is popular, easy to do, or simply requires little courage. The challenge to leadership comes when doing the right thing is unpopular, puts a goal at risk, protects an employee from changing his behavior, or gives the person making the decision an easier alternative that is not the right decision.

What kind of twentieth-century challenges and decisions are we talking about? What examples can we cite that provide evidence of a lack of courage to do the right thing?

Let me ask a few questions—questions that are hard to answer because the answer is not popular.

- Would we have labor unions today if management had dealt with its employees fairly and in a win-win manner over the course of the last 100 years?
- Would we have minimum wage legislation if the decisions to pay our employees fairly without taking advantage of them had been the norm?
- Would we have autocratic or authoritarian managers if we insisted on treating our employees the way *we* wanted to be talked to and treated?
- Do we believe in our corporate values to the degree that we would actually require our top technical employee or top salesperson to adhere to them? Do we make them the exception as long as they produce?
- Why do we have mandatory safety training that requires government agencies to ensure compliance?
- Why must we conduct ethics training, sexual harassment education, and equal employment seminars?

Unfortunately, the answers are unpleasant to hear. We have done it to ourselves. After generations of power and control being exercised by a few at the top, and many too weak to fight the system below them, we have a business environment that is full of distrust and legislation.

Why? Our "leaders" believed their own propaganda—that they were in control and had the power to do whatever they wanted to do. In essence, they failed to do the right thing. Many likely believed they were doing the right thing. The right thing would have been for them to ask why the increased legislation? The increased distrust? The decline in employee morale? The decline in teamwork? Why is a handshake no longer a contract? Excuses are plentiful, but the right thing was not modeled.

As leaders, we must always be willing to ask ourselves, "What is the right thing?"

The Perfect Leader warns us to continue to ask the 'right thing' question.

> Colossians 2:8 "See to it that no one takes you captive through hollow and deceptive philosophy, which depends on human tradition and the basic principles of this world rather than on Christ."

The courage to do the right thing is void of blame. There is no one else to pin the failure on—no C.Y.A. (cover your "ankles"), no circumstance, or situation that will neutralize our responsibility and accountability.

COURAGE AND CONTROVERSY

Show me a person who does not have some controversy surrounding him, no one second-guessing him, and who has constant harmony, and I'll show you a person who is doing nothing of significance. For sure, he is not leading with courage.

There is no better example of this evidence than The Perfect Leader himself. Here was a person with all the necessary skills, knowledge, and attitudes to lead with total wisdom and execution. Yet controversy surrounded his life on a daily basis.

This brings forward an important dimension. A leader can be strong, do the right thing, follow a sound philosophy, and model the right values and still be criticized and live in frequent controversy.

Before we pass off the controversy surrounding us as an unfair or inaccurate accusation, it would be important to validate our action as the right thing. If we are rationalizing our actions, then we have fallen into the trap of self-acceptance. We must be careful to watch our patterned behavior and avoid making excuses for our actions under the guise of "That's just me."

As The Perfect Leader so capably modeled, be willing to go to the mat on the major issues. Stand up and put a stake in the ground. Be a leader of principle. The flip side is also appropriate at times. Be willing to empathize, and be kind. Avoid creating controversy on trivial pursuits that result in little change, but damage the relationship or reputation.

COURAGE AND LIFELONG LEARNING

There are many benefits of leaders acting with courage, but none are as beneficial as the legacy and example they leave for future generations and other less experienced leaders.

Think of the great leaders who have left their marks on our government, businesses, churches, athletics, and families. What a shame it would have been if their courageous acts were never observed and recorded. Not only would a national treasure have been lost, but also the opportunity to learn from example would be gone forever. This can serve as great encouragement to each leader.

No better example of life-long learning exists than to study the work, deeds, and words of The Perfect Leader. He left this legacy to us by his intent and on-purpose behavior.

> I Peter 2:21 & 23 "To this you were called, because Christ suffered for you, *leaving you an example, that you should follow in his steps.* When they hurled their insults at him, he did not retaliate; when he suffered, he made no threats . . ."

CHAPTER SEVEN

PERFECT LEADER QUALITY #7:
DEVELOPER OF PEOPLE

As discussed earlier, the focus of management and the focus of leadership are different. While both skills are required in today's business environment, it is indeed rare for a single individual to have innate talents in both arenas. However, this does not mean we cannot learn both skill sets.

Management is primarily focused on how to control the resources under its charge. These resources include money, technology, equipment, schedules and, of course, people. It is this focus and control that leads to many of the problems business is experiencing today. In reality, control is not the villain, but the way in which control is used is at fault.

In order to manage the people resource, certain tools and skills are required. Over the years, managers have been asked to direct, delegate, control, motivate, budget, schedule, decision make, and problem solve.

These skills certainly helped us grow our business—the financial and product side at least. However, the very things that helped us to produce more product and volume, and therefore add more people, seldom helped us mature our own employees.

The case can be made that by delegating more responsibility to an individual, the person will develop automatically. While there is some truth to this, the reality is that the individual will likely develop himself through constant trial and error. This is hardly an efficient or strategic method.

Left with a realization that the manager did little to help, the employee views the manager as giving more work and seldom giving any praise or recognition. In fact, if the employee is a high performer, he has likely found his manager unavailable since the manager is spending most of his time on task related problems and the low performers.

This brings us to why leadership is so crucial to business. We need the focus that leadership brings in order to revive the human spirit in the workplace and return our work to the role of providing a sense of worth and satisfaction. Our businesses, government, and families need the trust, inspiration, and hope that leadership provides.

Leadership must create an atmosphere and enough magnetism that people will want to follow its lead. While leaders are perfectly aware that control is necessary to be able to repeat successes, they are not insistent that they are the ones in control. They actually gain this control through empowering their followers while making a conscious effort to develop their skills, knowledge, attitude, and experiences.

While the focus in this chapter is development, a quick understanding of empowerment is appropriate. Development and empowerment are like salt and pepper. They are separate but related. Both add seasoning to the individual's growth. One without the other can leave the follower with very low job satisfaction.

Few words are more misunderstood or create more anxiety with traditional managers than "empowerment."

The important thing to remember is that empowerment can only be provided by those with control to give. Secondly, it is a choice to empower someone.

The following formula has helped many of my clients to understand that they are in control of empowerment and what must be provided by their leadership to empower one of their followers.

Empowerment = Direction X Autonomy X Support

The leader is responsible for providing direction to his follower. Direction is the framework for empowerment. It includes the vision, mission, values, strategies, and goals of the organization. In addition, it is helpful for the individual to know the role and responsibilities he will be asked to fulfill. If the person operates within this framework, the leader can trust that the individual is operating in the same arena as the leader.

Autonomy consists of a scale ranging from no autonomy to full autonomy. This is earned through the individual's track record of performance, the level of experience, and maturity in an area he has demonstrated. Finally, the leader must take into account the person's skills, knowledge, and attitudes.

Support is the assessment of what the individual needs and expects in the area of help required. It should be evaluated in regard to the individual's personality, experience, and the size or risk of the task to be accomplished. In addition, the leader must be willing to be available and remove any barriers beyond the control of the individual.

Finally, remember that each of the factors is connected by a multiplier and not an addition sign. The absence of any of the factors renders a formula of zero empowerment.

WILLINGNESS: WALK OR TALK?

The key to developing people is willingness. If an individual is to be one of your key lieutenants, then his development is far too critical an assignment to delegate this responsibility to someone other than yourself. Others may assist and actually add value and knowledge, but the essence and heart and soul of leadership can only be imbedded by the leader.

The previous paragraph likely has many of the readers saying, "This is obvious. Why is this even worth the time to put it in print?" Quite simply, talking development and doing development are worlds apart. No one can argue with the logic; but real development is an extreme commitment of time, energy, and rearranging priorities.

Industry standards indicate that it takes twenty-four months to develop a first-line supervisor. This assumes effective managerial support and follow-up. Seldom do salespeople carry their own weight through their first two years. We spend twelve years in school just to get the foundation. So why should we believe this is a part-time exercise? During twenty years of consulting, I doubt that I have met twenty-five leaders who would be classified as "a developer of their subordinates." Many make the claim and many give focused efforts for a while, but few really believe this is one of their core responsibilities. This is true by measuring their daily actions.

Have you ever stopped to ask why we need formal mentoring programs, formal succession plans, or formal employee development plans? The answer is painstakingly clear; we talk development, but don't walk development. It simply takes too much time and focus.

In addition, we developed our main skill set in developing things, not people. So most of us are more comfortable with tasks than relationships.

As a coach, I was rewarded for win-loss record, championships, and attendance. I was neither rewarded nor acknowledged for how many players developed into college players or became model citizens in our community because of the lessons they developed through athletics. The focus was clearly on things, not people.

The Perfect Leader gives us a haunting revelation of how critical He believed the development of his twelve primary followers was to be in regard to the fulfillment of his vision and mission. He spent three years (nearly twenty-four hours a day) with them—teaching, listening, coaching, counseling, correcting, and challenging them—instructing them himself. No wonder his vision and mission are alive and well two thousand years later.

No one is suggesting this type of commitment today.

However, we can't expect real development when we are lucky to devote two hours a month to our high-potential subordinates.

We do have a leadership crisis today. Are you willing to do anything about it? Check your last three month's calendar to validate just how much time you have spent coaching, mentoring, and developing your key personnel.

STAGES OF DEVELOPMENT AND GROWTH

One of the most important pieces of knowledge that I have acquired is a model called the Growth Curve. This model puts into context the challenges and approaches that leaders face when attempting to meet the needs of a person they are trying to develop. While the model is far more complex than will be described in these pages and is not limited to individual growth only, it provides a valuable backdrop to examine a development strategy. I first was exposed to this model through my work with Wilson Learning Corporation, and I am using the model with their support. Many companies use a similar "S" curve to discuss business trends, product cycles, and personnel readiness.

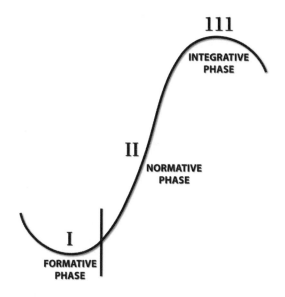

PHASE I

As one can see from the description of Phase I, this is an exciting yet traumatic time for the employee. Whether the employee is new to the job or simply new to the task, the circumstance is similar. He is excited to try something new and afraid to fail.

Employees are long on attitude and short on experience. Without a successful track record on this new assignment, the anxiety to show what they can do and their desire to validate "the leader's confidence in them" places them between a rock and a hard place.

I call this syndrome "ignorance on fire." The person is very gung-ho, but lacks the skills or savvy to get the job done. He also may be very reluctant to ask for help, as this may signal (in his mind) to the leader that he cannot handle this type of assignment.

The leader needs to address the approaches required for dealing with Phase I employees at this time. He should be direct and willing to tell the employee what to do to meet expectations and performance criteria. The leader must be willing to be specific and detailed about the assignments. Goals should be relatively simple and feedback must be frequent. This allows the employee to either gain reassurance that actions are on target or correct his action before the error is too far advanced to recover.

These actions build an employee's self-confidence and ability to perform so he can be a productive member of the team. The leader's ability to manage this assignment correctly and remain available to direct and provide support translates into how quickly the employee is a producer and is capable of being left to his own initiative.

The production and self-worth that is created in this phase is perhaps the most important benefit. The person that inspires him, demonstrates the follower's importance by giving of his time, and helps the follower succeed is without a doubt *earning the right to become his leader.*

It is said that we model many of the behaviors of our leaders.

Some years ago, I was visiting with a client in Tulsa, Oklahoma. He shared with me that he had recently been to one of the power plants he was responsible for managing. To his dismay, he observed behaviors that were not aligned with the approaches he believed to be required. He shared how concerned he was. What had he done to cause the employees to "model" his actions in this manner? Their actions were foreign to him.

While his conclusion was uncomfortable at a personal level, it also served to change the way he handled Phase I opportunities. He concluded that he delegated their development. While they worked for him, *he was not their leader.* What a painful learning experience, and it is one that cannot be undone.

Once the employee has demonstrated some consistency of performance and does not require the frequent direction and feedback, he progresses to Phase II.

PHASE II

Early Phase II is a period that typically provides personal satisfaction to the employee. He can handle additional responsibility and accountability. He usually sees this as a reward for his performance.

The employee is starting to feel confident; therefore, he feels independent from the frequent contact of the leader.

As this independence continues to grow, the leader must manage the employee differently than when he was in Phase I. To continue telling and directing the employee at this time will actually lead to the employee feeling over managed and under led. The outcome can be a damaged relationship and the beginning of job dissatisfaction.

The Perfect Leader recognized this and once the "followers" were into early Phase II, He provided more and more independence and empowerment. He was present and supportive in a different way—one in which his followers now exerted their independence by applying what they had been taught and had learned.

The Perfect Leader took approximately three years to fulfill this transfer of vision and mission. Why should today's leaders think they should be able to develop their followers in forty hours of training? Both corporate America and parents must recognize the development of our charges is not a one-time activity, done quickly, nor can it be done on the cheap.

The leader must now change his approach in regard to employee contact. The leader must now exploit his influence. The leader looks for the opportunity to coach and counsel, thereby utilizing the experience he has gained. To do this, the leader must display personal versatility. No longer can he just tell and direct. The employee has skills and confidence; therefore, the leader's core skills are centered on his ability to listen, question, and problem solve with the employee.

In addition, the employee does not need to see or hear from the leader as frequently. The leader now changes his approach to one of monitoring progress and giving specific feedback relative to the checkpoints.

It can be expected that an employee will progress in a Phase II state for many years. In time, the very thing that made the employee successful may in fact prevent his progression. Like most situations, it is easy to become complacent or think we don't need to learn or change to stay current and get better.

When this change begins to become a major factor, the employee has entered the late stage of Phase II. The needs and expectations of the employee and leader are about to change again. It is time for renewal. While often this change is met with resistance, there is no other alternative if the development of the employee is to continue.

This requirement for renewal signals a bifurcation (learning the new knowledge requirements and screening the old knowledge) and the entry into Phase III.

PHASE III

The employee's ability to learn and accept the new, while selectively pruning the old ways, is the key to the progression of the employee's development and career extension.

This phase creates a multitude of opportunities. As in all opportunities, there is great potential and great risk. The relationship between the leader and follower will be put to the test. A healthy relationship built on trust will enable both individuals to maximize their abilities, skills, and knowledge.

Poor relationships are magnified in this phase and frequently translate into disaster. It is very difficult to accomplish the changes and innovations needed if mutual respect and trust are lacking.

So how does the leader continue the development of the employee during this phase? As in the first two phases, the requirements of Phase III are also unique, and they demand the leader's flexibility to modify his approach.

Phase III requires people to attack problems in a collaborative manor. The skills and attitudes that make the employee productive and irreplaceable center on his ability to work interdependently.

Communication and presentation of ideas within a group or team setting are critical. What could be done independently now must be accomplished with others. Therefore, skills requiring participation, negotiation, team decision making, innovation, teamwork, and conflict resolution are critical to the success of the individual and organization.

The leader must display great courage, vision, and a willingness to empower his employees. His ability to provide a stabilizing force during all the chaos and change serves to reassure the employee, therefore, allowing him to be more at ease in doing the required work.

Finally, the leader must truly understand the need for empowering the follower at this stage. Innovation and risk-taking are critical skill sets and attitudes needed to survive this change and grow to a new, future state of welfare.

After years of being trained to eliminate mistakes, correct errors, and to act conservatively, the employee must trust the direction and intent of the leader. Otherwise, no new action will take place.

Unfortunately, I have experienced many of these "no new actions" taking place in business and government today. The result is prolonged decline and decay.

Leadership cannot command the employee to feel differently about the trust, support, and empowerment that is being promoted. He must be won over by consistent and frequent messages—followed by consistent actions being demonstrated by leadership.

The leadership must be willing to invest in the training to equip the employee to execute the new skills required. This takes place at a time when cost is usually under heavy scrutiny. Courage and doing the right thing come into play again.

THE TRANSITION TO NEW LEADERS

The leader must keep the vision and values in front of the followers at all times during the Phase III experience. During the changes taking place, at light speed, the vision and values serve to reinforce direction and provide stability.

The Perfect Leader once again leaves us with an example and model of this behavior. As one of His very last interactions with his chosen eleven followers, He reinforced his vision and directed their actions, while giving encouragement and support. Clearly, the baton is being passed, but of equal importance, the *followers are ready to lead. The new leaders have been developed.*

> Matthew 28:16–20 "Then the eleven disciples went to Galilee, to the mountain where Jesus had told them to go. When they saw him, they worshiped him; but some doubted. Then Jesus came

to them and said, "All authority in heaven and on earth has been given to me. Therefore go and make disciples of all nations, baptizing them in the name of the Father and of the Son and of the Holy Spirit, and teaching them to obey everything I have commanded you. And surely I am with you always, to the very end of the age."

He had trained and developed them. They shared his vision and values. They had seen his courage under fire. They watched Him work on purpose in everything He did. He had been available when they needed Him. He had taught them about the severity of consequences and did this while being supportive and encouraging. He had taken them from "ignorance on fire" to maturity, ready to use their unique talents in the pursuit of a common and shared vision. Finally, He forgave their mistakes and rewarded their successes. Why wouldn't this group be ready to step forward and assume the leadership challenge before them?

In conclusion, The Perfect Leader tells them He will be with them to the very end. This is impossible with today's constant relocations, early retirements, mergers, acquisitions, and rapid movement between jobs. Right? Wrong.

Each of us has been shaped by other leaders. A former coach of mine, Joe Caligure, greatly influenced my life. He lives 2000 miles away, and I have not seen him in 30 years. Another coach, Jim Stackpole, has passed away. Another, Bryant Curry, is retired and lives in another state.

Are these leaders still with me? Absolutely, I cannot forget what they taught me. It is hard to know if it was their teaching or my new learning that causes me to act. They are part of me; my every decision, my character, and my attitudes were shaped by these men. They live on in me and the realm of my influence on a daily basis and will continue to do so until the very end of my life. Thank goodness these men took the time to invest in me!

What will our sons, daughters, spouses, friends, bosses, coworkers, and employees say we "transfused" into them? I can only pray that the model of The Perfect Leader will one day be evident to them through my leadership. What is your legacy?

For me, I desire to be a "leadership virus," infecting and spreading the lessons The Perfect Leader has taught me and will continue to teach me—to all I contact, love, and care about.

CHAPTER EIGHT

PERFECT LEADER QUALITY #8:

FORGIVENESS OF IMPERFECT MOTIVES AND ACTIONS

"Then Peter came to Jesus and asked, "Lord, how many times shall I forgive my brother when he sins against me? Up to seven times?" Jesus answered, "I tell you, not seven times, but seventy-seven times."

Matthew 18:21–22

This is a great lesson from The Perfect Leader. He knew human nature was to harbor the wrongs and attempt to even the score. At the very least, we would keep track of how many times someone does something to us so we can feel justified in our retaliatory behavior—be it aggressive or passive. An act of revenge or harboring a grudge, either way the relationship is over.

A popular fable warns us to beware of the wronged man, for he is always seeking revenge.

No behavioral characteristic exhibited by The Perfect Leader is harder to understand, and therefore demonstrate, than true forgiveness.

Likewise, no other quality is more central to leadership.

I can hear all the conventional wisdom and teachings of our learned advisors.

"A leopard doesn't change its spots."
"Done once, shame on you. Done twice, shame on me."
"Kill or be killed."
"Keep your enemies very close or very far away."

Regardless, we all have tapes playing in our heads to protect us and warn us from being burned again. Like a spent match that cannot be ignited again, so our relationships seem to travel the path of no return. Due to the imperfection of our intentions and actions, we will relish in the dungeon of distrust forever. Nothing would do more to heal America's business problems, family problems, and civil challenges than a good dose of true mutual forgiveness.

INTENT VS DELIVERY

I often use a saying that the natural outcome of communication is miscommunication. With the complexity of today's business and personal environments, it is very difficult to explain our every intention. Even when we think we conveyed our intentions perfectly, we are surprised to hear how others interpreted the message. Like multiple witnesses at a car accident, they all saw the same wreck, but they all have their own eyewitness accounts.

Even if the intention could be explained perfectly, we then will never deliver the action as purposefully and clearly as intended.

This gives rise to the fact that people are often perceived as saying one thing while doing something different—often to their own surprise when they are made aware of how someone has interpreted their actions.

My experience in the consulting field has convinced me that few people really intend to do "ill-will" to others, initially. This often changes when someone feels he has been taken advantage of or stabbed in the back. Our real problem is that we are judged through the eyes of another person who most frequently is unsure of our intentions.

This comes down to a very simple question. What is required to give a person the benefit of the doubt concerning his actions and words?

The people I consider my personal leaders are given the benefit of the doubt, always. Why? I trust their intentions regardless of the imperfection of their actions (delivery). They are allowed additional time to make their plan work, see the result, or explain it in further detail. I am not waiting to call their attention to the first sign of deviation from the spoken path of the plan.

The Perfect Leader had the foresight to recognize that we do not forgive easily. Well over *one hundred* Scriptures are devoted to forgiveness and its derivatives. Do you think this is a lesson that is hard for us to learn, or could it be we don't want to learn it?

What would have been the consequence to The Perfect Leader's vision if He did not forgive? It would mean his values were words only and not a way of life. It would have meant the mistakes his young followers made would have received strong and frequent chastisement. Their mistakes would be part of their "performance portfolio" and be with them for life, always available for recall when a lesson or grievance needed to be expressed. His whole life and example would have taken on a different meaning. There would be no "movement" continuing 2000 years later.

The Perfect Leader had proof that some of the people intended Him harm and still He forgave.

When The Perfect Leader was set up with false charges and judged guilty to appease the public pressure, He still forgave, even though He knew it would lead to his death.

> Luke 23:34 " . . . Father, forgive them, for they do
> not know what they are doing . . ."

He knew some were doing this with full, conscious knowledge, while others were caught up in the moment, following the crowd, or just lacked the personal courage to take a different stand. He also knew that none were able to realize the long and lasting impact (consequence) of their actions. It made no difference; His statement forgave all of the involved party regardless of their intentions or actions.

The lesson is clear. If we take the responsibility of leadership, there will be some who want us to fail or to be destroyed. That is part one of the lesson.

Lesson two is equally simple. It is not worth the internal impact on ourselves that the worry and anxiety will generate. Instead, focus on our vision, values, and mission. Pay attention to followers, and don't get side tracked while focusing unduly on detractors. Keeping our focus and doing the right thing while defending ourselves, harboring a grudge, or being distracted with another person is extremely difficult.

Leaders have the ability to focus on the things they can influence and control. Once again, The Perfect Leader coaches us on how to prepare and occupy our minds. He understands clearly the linkage of our thoughts to our actions.

> Philippians 4:8–9 "Finally, brothers, whatever is true, whatever is noble, whatever is right, whatever is pure, whatever is lovely, whatever is admirable–if anything is excellent or praiseworthy–think about such things. Whatever you have learned or received or heard from me, or seen in me–put it into practice. And the God of peace will be with you."

If we were to think about what the Scripture told us to think about and do what it told us to do, what would our actions be?

Nowhere does The Perfect Leader tell us to plot revenge, take time to worry about what others are doing to us, etc. He does tell us to be wise and seek counsel before we act (Proverbs 5:1–2; Proverbs 4:5–6; Proverbs 15:22).

Even when a conflict is required, the advice is clear. Focus and prepare.

Proverbs 20:18 "Make plans by seeking advice; if you wage war, obtain guidance."

HIGH STANDARDS WILL REQUIRE FORGIVENESS

The Perfect Leader set very high standards for his followers and Himself alike. When standards are high, and the people carrying them out are less skilled than required or inexperienced with the new levels of expectation, there will be shortcomings and failures. This should be understood and expected. What to do and how to do it when these occur should be part of the initial planning. Consequences for actions should not be established after the actions are history. Consequences represent the rewards and punishment equation.

Even The Perfect Leader had to deal with the lack of experience and skills of his followers. The experience and skills are in respect to the purpose for which He called them. He likely felt the same frustration and disappointment we do as our employees fall short of the desired target, make a simple task much harder than it really should have been, and fail to ask for help before stepping off the deep end.

However, it is through the trials, mistakes, and failures that our full learning can grow and take root deep inside our being. This also creates an opportunity for the leader. The way these situations are handled creates a link from the leader to the follower. A leader who is always hard on these matters soon creates followers that are timid and too cautious—maybe even afraid. The leader who ignores the shortcomings on a frequent basis will communicate that just trying is good enough; high standards are neither achievable nor real . . . just words.

The Perfect Leader had many frustrations of this type. His followers just did not understand some situations. Sometimes, they did things the wrong way. Sometimes they fell short of the expectations.

In any event, The Perfect Leader handled the situations, in

light of their unique personalities and their phases of development, with actions consistent to the values.

The followers learned his commitment to them and the vision He supported. He had followers for life. Incidentally, of the eleven who assumed the leadership, nine of the eleven were martyred. However, they had developed leaders to take their places. So even in the face of disaster, their preparation ensured the continuity of the vision. Thus, the saga continues today.

THE TRUST PARADOX

I am still amazed at how often my clients are taken back by the lack of trust that has been allowed to fester over the years. It speaks volumes about our history of management, employee relations, and our lack of real communication with each other.

In defense of these same clients, many have inherited the "baggage" from previous management; *previous* decisions and interactions are *now* what they have to live with. Regardless, the changes that are required today take mutually shared responsibility and vision. These cannot be mandated, even in "going out of business" scenarios. We must understand the remedy and be willing to execute it if we are to leverage the resources within our organizations.

In the twenty-plus years I have been working with management, I can honestly say I have met very few individuals who were not intending to work in the employee's best interest initially. Like the employee, management can also be personally hurt and become bitter or revengeful. However, nearly all are interested in healing the wounds.

The shock and realization of the problem usually surfaces during the announcement and rollout of a new competitive initiative, the very initiative that requires the support and commitment of the employee.

It is believed (by management) that because management is "in-the-know" its intentions are honorable and in the best interest of the enterprise, and the employee will follow with vigor and energy.

Because our history in management has been to provide information on a need-to-know basis, and we have been very selective in what is shared, the perception of something being hidden exists. Baggage exists with both parties.

I know of only one solution. It is relatively painless and requires no new skills. It does, however, take great courage and confidence.

To get the "old baggage" off the train, simply make a decision to throw it off. Get the people who were involved in putting it on the train and ask them to share in the act of throwing the baggage off.

During the teen years of our children, my wife Pam came up with a unique way to reduce guilt, tension, and potential mistrust between "the kids" and "the parents." Every four to six months, we would hold an "amnesty night."

Essentially, each of our children was given the opportunity to share something that he knew was outside the range of Pam's and my approval. This "load," once confessed, was forgiven immediately. It afforded them the opportunity to reduce the blackmail that their fellow siblings held over their heads and to exercise a "get out of jail free" card with their parents.

The idea was originally met with skepticism, but it eventually flourished and actually became a fun event. There were two over-arching requirements. First, there had to be total, unconditional forgiveness, regardless what was shared. Second, it could never be used or brought up again in the communication or discipline. Our grown children have implemented plans for such an event in their own families. Today we can share in some mutual stories and laughs, which if handled in a traditional manner could have served to divide us.

In our complex world, with multiple problems and temptations facing our children, we learned a lot about our parenting—where we often were too trusting or asleep at the wheel.

We not only created a forum for trust, but we became better communicators and parents.

Declaring to forgive each other for accidental or purposeful wrongs is the key. It can be a new beginning, immediately. In addition, it is much less painful than rehashing the old situations, placing blame, and tearing the scabs off old wounds.

Forgiveness requires courage and a willingness to be vulnerable. The first step rests on the shoulders of the leader.

If the leader does not forgive first, it is certain the employee will not initiate the interaction or mutual forgiveness.

WE ARE ALL JUDGMENTAL

At the root of the problem is a basic reality of human nature. We are all judgmental of others, and we base our judgments on our own comfort zone and personal behaviors. Therefore, if I require a lot of data to feel comfortable making a decision and want ample time to feel it is the best possible alternative, then I will expect or impose this behavior on others. The result? If you are comfortable with little data and make decisions quickly, I will not only be "uncomfortable" with your decision, but I may feel it is not thought through and likely wrong. The opposite scenario is also true.

All of these little interpersonal nuances create a high potential for misunderstandings and evaluations of intent and delivery.

The Perfect Leader provides some sobering thoughts for us.

> Luke 6:36–38 "Be merciful, just as your Father is merciful. Do not judge, and you will not be judged. Do not condemn, and you will not be condemned. Forgive, and you will be forgiven. Give, and it will be given to you."

The passage suggests some very lofty values for leaders to strive to obtain and integrate within their organization.

- ◆ Be merciful.
- ◆ Do not judge.
- ◆ Do not condemn.
- ◆ Give.
- ◆ Forgive.

The key to the entire message is the target—me—the only one I have control over. It is not for the "others," who need to clean up their acts to be worthy of my mercy, forgiveness, and gifts. We cannot wait for the follower to initiate the first step in healing the wounds. This is a leadership function.

The situation reminds me of a lifelong lesson I learned at the tender age of twenty-two. My wife and I were living in Alamogordo, New Mexico, where I was teaching and serving as the high school baseball coach.

During this time, we were "adopted" by a couple from our church whose son happened to play on one of my teams. They became our family, since we knew no one when we moved. As a result, the Rumseys asked us to attend a reception for their twenty-fifth anniversary.

In one of my "ignorance on fire" moments, I asked Loretta, "What do you attribute as the key to twenty-five years of wedded bliss?"

Without hesitating, she said, "I do 75 percent of all the work." To say the least, I was dumbfounded and speechless. To think she would take all the credit! I was moving rapidly to my most internal judgment. My nonverbal behavior must have given me away because she smiled and added, "Terry, Atwell does the other 75 percent."

This was truly one of the best lessons of my life. I learned that if we are willing to meet people only halfway, and if either of us fails to go the entire "halfway," we will never meet. There will always be a gap, which I will likely believe to be the other person's fault.

If the leader will go 75 percent of the way in forgiveness,

the chance that the problem will be resolved is much greater. Why not 100 percent? Simply stated, forgiveness involves two people, therefore, two decisions. We must count on the truth in the Luke 6:36–38 passage.

DELIVERING NEGATIVE CONSEQUENCES

The Perfect Leader would not be the perfect leader if He avoided dealing with poor performance and attitude.

No one likes the role of disciplinarian. However, it is one of the responsibilities that leaders inherit when they take the assigned role of leader.

Negative consequences are the result of previous behavior and are a major source of individuals becoming disenchanted with the leader. Many feel they have legitimate excuses, or they are being singled out. Some feel they are being treated differently than others in similar situations. The bottom-line, this is a high-risk activity for the leader. In many ways, it is a no win situation where you feel "danged if you do and danged if you don't."

The Perfect Leader was frequently faced with having to communicate and deliver messages and consequences that were caused by someone's poor performance or attitude.

The task, while not pleasant, can be handled professionally and with wisdom. This provides the required accountability, while allowing the person to escape with his dignity and not feel personally attacked.

With all the positive situations The Perfect Leader provides for our education, it is a fact that He also had to dismiss one of his original, hand-chosen twelve followers. He challenged the teachers of the law, provided straight messages to the rich and poor, and delivered clear consequences to government officials as well as the politicians of the day.

In reviewing the wisdom behind the delivery, several consistent behaviors emerge across all the situations.

1.   He was always *compassionate*. It is obvious that He truly cared for the people He was talking to. He was hard on the issue and took no middle ground. At the same time, He delivered the message without malice or personal attack.

2.   He was always *empathetic*. He had an ability to look through the eyes of those He was talking to. Be it the teachers of the law, the tax collectors, the rich, young ruler, or the prostitute at the well, He made people believe that He understood their circumstances. While not condoning the behavior, He was available to help them.

3.   He set the model for delivering a *consistent message that was understandable to the listener.* His use of stories to illustrate the point, his accurate reference to the prophesy, and his simple, brief message helped people to clearly hear and relate it to themselves.

Just as there were consistent behaviors in how He communicated the consequences, there were also four steps to each of his messages.

1.   The message was very clearly and concisely delivered.

2.   He found a way to repeat it. It sometimes took the form of a parable; sometimes the message was repeated in other messages, but it was always repeated and consistent.

3.   The consequences, either positive or negative, were very clear. Sometimes both positive and negative consequences were articulated. People were given choices.

4.   He was always fair and consistent in delivering the outcomes.

The Perfect Leader recognized that it would be difficult for his followers to model this behavior, so He gave them a little encouragement, clear direction, and a bottom-line result for their effort.

Colossians 3:12–13 " . . . clothe yourselves with compassion, kindness, humility, gentleness and patience. Bear with each other and forgive whatever grievances you may have against one another. Forgive as the Lord forgave you."

How interesting that even with compassion, kindness, humility, gentleness, and patience, we will still be pushed to our limit. He tells us to "just hang in there" and make it an act of will. Others do not need to be deserving of the forgiveness, but they will never follow us if we do not first take this step. The word "grievances" is also plural, which indicates a number of problems, and it apparently goes both ways since He indicates in the phrase "against one another."

Verse 14 ends with these words, "all together in perfect harmony." Nice result!

While there are many more examples that could be used to illustrate this leadership characteristic of The Perfect Leader, He makes the consequence very clear in these final two directives.

In the Lord's Prayer, He reminds us, "Forgive us our debts, *as we* forgive our debtors." This is perhaps one of the most quoted and known passages in the Bible.

Before the last reference is made in this chapter, it may be interesting to see what the Thesaurus says in response to the word forgiveness. The words used to describe this term include: the act to forgive, absolution, pardon, mercy, exoneration, reprieve, and remission.

What would our businesses, homes, schools, governments, and society be like with just a little more forgiveness? All the education in the world will not heal our hurts. How far would a little mutual forgiveness go?

Followers won't start it.

High standards, consistency, courage, and fairness were discussed earlier in this chapter. Leadership is also responsible for setting and communicating the positive and negative consequences and for acting or failing to act on the direction requested.

One of the positive consequences discussed was "perfect unity." Others are clear in other passages. The negative consequences are also spelled out. Remember, forgiveness does not take skills; it takes courage and a willingness (attitude) to act. We control this decision ourselves, which makes the final passage of this chapter very sobering.

The Perfect Leader warns *all* involved.

> Colossians 3:25 "Anyone who does wrong will be repaid for his wrong, and there is no favoritism."

I interpret the message as it is wrong not to forgive. We pay one way now or another way later, but payment will come.

CHAPTER NINE

PERFECT LEADER QUALITY #9:
EVER THE ENCOURAGER

"The Lord your God is with you, he is mighty to save.
He will take great delight in you, he will quiet you
with his love, he will rejoice over you with singing."

Zephaniah 3:17

Zephaniah was a "follower" of The Perfect Leader. What a powerful endorsement he gives about the power of encouragement he receives from his leader. So heartfelt that he can communicate the confidence he feels to others. I wonder how Zephaniah felt to have his "leader" take great delight in him, to be calming with his very attitude, or to be excited that he was his follower. This has certainly not been my experience.

Looking back on the twentieth century reminds us of how much change has taken place. A newspaper was conducting a poll on the most significant happenings of the century. As expected, the Atomic Bomb, the World Wars, the landing on the moon, and various medical and technological breakthroughs topped the list. It caused me to think about my opinion of the most significant happening. I chose speed.

Today we can e-mail across the world in seconds, drive cars capable of reaching well over 100 mph, get live telecast while the wars are being fought, fly anywhere in a matter of hours, send packages all around the world overnight, etc. We live in a world of speed and seldom stop to see or feel its impact.

Is it surprising that the word stress is a twentieth-century word? Not only was it coined recently, it is a major cause of physical and psychological illnesses.

Speed also raises the bar concerning how we should perform and how much we should accomplish in an hour, day, month, or year. My clients are accustomed to setting tough goals and then adding "stretch" goals on top of them. The real goals become the stretch goals, requiring more performance in the same time as allotted to their original goals.

We put our whole family to work to keep up with the rat race. We enroll our kids in every possible formal activity that comes along and still expect to give quality time to work, family, church, community, self, and spouse. The days of having everyone at a staff meeting or at the dinner table have disappeared.

We have been lulled by speed. Work harder and faster, retire early, and find additional time somewhere. No wonder the projections reach figures of 30 percent when discussions of mental fatigue, depression, anxiety, and illness are communicated by the medical experts when describing the workforce in U.S. industry. People complain of no relief, burnout, panic attacks, and stress.

The time for encouragement is long overdue. Not a small measured dose, but an immersion. I want a leader who is interested in me as a person, not just as a worker. As Zephaniah related, a leader who "delights, quiets, and rejoices" would encourage me beyond measure. (A follower with those same traits would be pretty exciting as well.)

Most everyone has too much to do, too many responsibilities and too little time to accomplish their assignments. Nothing helps you reset your mind for the upcoming day of additional challenges like sincere appreciation and encouragement. When we, as leaders, become too busy, our focus changes to what's on our plate. There is an increased risk that we will forget to inform our partners how much their efforts are appreciated, and we won't give those brief words of encouragement.

"I do not have to tell people thanks. That is why they get paid." This axiom is old school and does not even faintly resemble leadership.

I enjoyed Tom Brokaw's book on *The Greatest Generation.* However, I am far from giving this generation a grade of "A." Most of the problems our families, businesses, and the government itself experience and try to fix *today* were left to us by unintentional neglect while under the watch of yesterday's leaders. While I give them an A+ rating in saving the world from Hitler and defending our way of life, this focus neglected other leadership responsibilities.

We are encumbered with legislation. We have every legal watchdog agency imaginable that drives our paperwork, taxes, and time to an unmatchable level. We have horrendous trust issues between employees and management. We work five and a half months each year just to pay our taxes. We were not taught how to cheer for our soldiers. We never started to deal with prejudices, race, or corruption in our own government. We used up the environment and degraded it in the name of profit. Leadership is not limited to a few, highly visible areas but to all arenas of our life. No one leader has the skills, following, time, or energy to be a leader in all arenas. In my opinion, the greatest weakness of the "Greatest Generation" was that they created few visible leaders and many followers. By intent and design, they managed and manufactured products, not a culture of leadership. This is a major reason we have a leadership crisis today in our families, churches, jobs, and government. The Greatest Generation receives an "A" in protecting the world from the tyranny of the Axis powers. However, in continuing to shape leaders to do the right thing in all aspects, they fell short. That was not the model established by The Perfect Leader. I give them a "B" overall for missing such an important element in developing future leaders.

Even former President Ronald Reagan addressed the bureaucracy his generation created in his 1981 Inaugural address. "In this present crisis, government is not the solution to our problem, government is the problem. If no one among us is capable of governing himself, then who among us has the capacity to govern someone else?" The people in power, the Greatest Generation, had allowed the problem of 1981 to exist.

This is not intended to be sour grapes or an excuse for our behavior today; it is to illustrate the point that if we become like our leaders, we will fail. We must lead and create many leaders.

What will the next generation say about us? Will we even get a "B"?

MY GREAT ENCOURAGER

As a young man, I coached basketball and baseball at the local high school. This resulted in my arriving home in the early evening. My toddler daughter, Kim, would come running to greet me as I entered the front door. What a welcome! I would scoop her up, put her on my shoulders, and start galloping around our family room; she would laugh and scream with excitement.

In reality, I was tired from a strenuous day, and without the greeting, I would have likely plopped down on the couch, happy to get off my feet. However, I had Annie Oakley on my shoulders. I was her "horsey." As with any stallion, I would get tired after a few minutes of galloping, then I would slow down. Then I would stop. Then the great encourager took over.

She would lean over and pucker up as I turned my head toward her; she would plant a big kiss squarely on my lips. She had given her horsey some sugar, and with this renewed encouragement, she would settle back for another gallop around the family room. This "give the horsey sugar" routine continued for years. She had learned that a little encouragement gave the "horsey" new energy and extended her fun.

This same little girl is now a grown woman, and without exception, she greets me with a kiss and says good-bye with a kiss. The "horsey," long since retired, is still getting the encouragement that bonded a relationship thirty years earlier.

Today she is still the person, other than my wife, who checks regularly to see what I'm doing, whether I need help or not, and sends me cards and other reminders that communicate to me that I count and that I am important. The "horsey" keeps on galloping.

With the right encouragement, we can contribute and perform well beyond our current mental and physical limits.

We have experienced a new energy source—encouragement.

BREAK THE "TOO MUCH" PARADIGM

Many of the management practices and philosophies used today are a carryover from the previous management generation. While many still serve us well, when it comes to attention, praise, and encouragement, our former managers were misled.

The old practices advocated focusing one's attention on the poor performers. Therefore, the heavy percentage of feedback was punitive, critical, or negative. In addition, the focus was to identify what wasn't working or what was broke and to fix it. Many careers blossomed as the troubleshooter went from assignment to assignment, fixing certain problems (nearly always task-focused) and creating other problems (nearly always relational in nature) for someone else to inherit and address later.

Praise was a seldom-used strategy or reward. When given, it was dealt out like gold to a very few, in small amounts, and infrequently. The common belief of management was to stay removed from the employees because friendships were for social, not professional, environments. Besides, if praise was given too often, people come to expect it and would take advantage of you. This practice became part of the "Theory X" form of management.

Finally, the issue of encouragement was viewed as fundamentally not required. People were hired to work; as a result, they received fair compensation. That was all management was required to do. The "soft stuff" had no bottom-line pay-off, and it was the job of human resources.

If you review the last four paragraphs, it is obvious that the term management, not leadership, is used. Historically, we have given an honorary leadership title to management. In reality, the behavior demonstrated was not leadership as it relates to people; it was, in fact, traditional management. Today, people do not want to follow individuals who are critical, seldom encouraging, and infrequently lets them know when they do something good. They may work for them, but don't forget, they choose their leaders; they inherit their managers.

The Perfect Leader clearly communicates that encouragement should be done frequently. In fact, He directs his followers to encourage one another daily.

> Hebrews 3:13 "But encourage one another daily,
> as long as it is called Today, so that none of you
> may be hardened by sin's deceitfulness."

It is interesting that The Perfect Leader commands us to encourage each other daily. The first letter in Today is capitalized, indicating that it represents every day of the week. He is not concerned with giving "too much" encouragement. In fact, his concern is with giving too little.

To be an encourager, we must have a focus outside our own problems and activities. We must observe another person on a regular basis and be able to discern when there is doubt, confusion, fear, disappointment, discouragement, or apprehension beginning to enter into the person's behavior.

We must learn to ask more questions, listen for the words, and read the body language that discloses that a little encouragement and support would be appreciated or needed.

None of this is possible if we do not first observe and understand what the individual's normal daily behavior looks like. Good leaders are students of their follower's words and actions. Like a thermometer, they are able to detect the slightest variation in their follower, signaling that something is out of the norm.

Throughout The Perfect Leader's life, we can observe Him

as an observer of people. Whether it was speaking to the little children, suggesting his disciples should rest, or acknowledging the pain in a person's talk or behavior, He clearly took the time to encourage all those around Him. Think about it. How hard is it to follow someone who legitimately cares, takes the time to listen, and encourages us at the personal level?

I have attempted to communicate to the executives I have coached over the years to monitor their employees' feedback and dialogue. If, *at a minimum,* they are not saying at least two positive and encouraging things for every negative thing they communicate, then they will develop more of a reputation as a manager than as a leader.

It is of interest to me that college and professional athletes thank their mothers, while seldom thanking their fathers when they are being interviewed. Why do you suppose this is the case? Could it be that their mother was more encouraging, while their father was more concerned with other demonstrated behavior, like performance? Regardless, it is obvious that the great majority do select their mothers for acknowledgement. The athlete must have benefited from this behavior and is now using the opportunity to repay a kindness.

The purpose of encouragement

The Perfect Leader knew that people would need to be encouraged frequently and in many different ways if they were to stay the course and achieve great things.

Before researching the Scriptures for this book, I must admit to overlooking the importance of encouragement as a critical daily behavior. It was ever so clear, in one form or another, that The Perfect Leader encouraged in every act and message recorded. The key Scripture that brings this to light is found in Romans 15:4.

> "For everything that was written in the past was written to teach us, so that through endurance and

the encouragement of the Scriptures we might
have hope."

According to this passage, the purpose of encouragement is
to provide hope. Which one of us does not need to feel there
is hope? We need hope to accomplish an assignment, hope to
achieve a difficult goal, hope for healing of a loved one, hope to
survive a destructive relationship, hope as we raise our teenag-
ers, hope to preserve our marriage, hope to meet our financial
needs, hope to take a courageous risk, or just hope to get up the
next morning to fight another day? Without hope, there is no
feeling that we can or will endure.

The Perfect Leader gives us a picture of when encouragement is required and how it can change our ultimate feelings
to press on. None of us is immune to the trials, challenges, and
tribulations of life. However, with someone encouraging us, we
can handle and manage incredible assignments and difficulties.

My family is good to observe my skills, talents, and actions.
However, it is the encouragement and support of my wife, Pam,
that is truly the rudder on my speedboat. Without her encouragement, some things in life would be too tough or simply too
unrewarding to pursue.

As I read this Scripture, it sounds all too familiar. At times,
as a small business owner, husband, and father, I must admit
to feeling pressed on every side, perplexed, persecuted, and on
occasion, struck down. The Perfect Leader says that through his
encouragement we have hope.

> II Corinthians 4:8–9 "We are hard pressed on
> every side, but not crushed; perplexed, but not
> in despair; persecuted, but not abandoned; struck
> down, but not destroyed."

With encouragement, there is hope.

Why encourage daily?

We never know all that a person is experiencing or how he
is interpreting the events and circumstances in his life. Even the

most confident people have doubts. Like the commercial that reminds the person to "never let 'em see you sweat," we have learned to put on the "no problem" mask. Often a reinforcing word of encouragement is the key to pressing on with conviction.

I am seldom negative, depressed, or doubtful that a problem cannot be resolved or an opportunity seized. However, it is very critical that on those occasions when I feel "pressed on every side, perplexed, and struck down" that someone recognizes that encouragement, not criticism, will be the activity that will lead me to action and success.

Often the people we expect to be the most encouraging are the very ones who magnify the problem and are critical with their actions and words. The leader must not fall into the trap of missing the need for their followers to feel encouraged so they can act.

The book of Job provides a vivid illustration of a person who is being pressed on every side and in every situation. The very people he would expect to encourage and provide hope make the situation more difficult by their critical nature and words.

> Job 2:9 "His wife said to him, "Are you still holding on to your integrity? Curse God and die!"

Later in the chapter, his friends spend seven days and seven nights with him without saying a single word to him. When they did begin to talk, they reminded him of all the negatives in his life and all the trials he was going through. These are friends?

Job gives a powerful and chastising speech to these "supporters."

> Job 16:2–5 "I have heard many things like these; miserable comforters are you all! Will your long-winded speeches never end? What ails you that you keep on arguing?

I also could speak like you . . . But my mouth would encourage you; comfort from my lips would bring you relief."

It is obvious that his wife and friends understood nothing about encouragement or its importance to the pressed, perplexed, and struck down. Unfortunately, too often our leadership can look and feel like what Job's friends supplied versus what Job needed.

There are more than fifty biblical references to derivatives of the word encouragement. Its use in a variety of situations will refresh our understanding of when it could be required. The following list is not intended to be all-inclusive, but it is to remind us of the many opportunities and circumstances in which encouragement can make a person feel like pressing forward and continuing the effort.

- Isaiah 1:17   Encourage the oppressed.
- I Thessalonians 3:2   Encourage to strengthen.
- I Thessalonians 5:11   Encourage to build up.
- I Thessalonians 5:14   Encourage the timid.
- II Thessalonians 2:16–17   Encourage to provide hope.
- Titus 2:6   Encourage the young.
- II Samuel 19:7   Encourage your team.
- Joshua 1:9   Encourage to be courageous.
- Psalms 56:3–4   Encourage to overcome fear.

As is evidenced by these Scriptures, we, as leaders, must make encouragement a way of life. In the complex and ever changing time we live in, every day has many problems. The Perfect Leader reminds us and encourages us to stay clear in our thinking.

> Matthew 6:25–26, 34 "Therefore I tell you, do not worry about your life, what you will eat or drink; or about your body, what you will wear. Is not life more important than food, and the body more important than clothes? Look at the birds of the air; they do not sow or reap or store away in barns, and yet your heavenly Father feeds them.

Are you not much more valuable than they? Who of you by worrying can add a single hour to his life? . . . Therefore do not worry about tomorrow, for tomorrow will worry about itself. Each day has enough trouble of its own."

While writing this chapter, I learned that a friend and business associate of mine was notified of the suicide of his 23-year-old son. I believe this friend to be a fine person and father, so his grief must be unbearable. I cannot help but wonder if someone, *anyone,* noticed or took the time to offer an encouraging word to this young man. I bet he was worried about tomorrow and did not see any hope. The Perfect Leader would not have missed the opportunity to encourage him. As a result, my friend might still have his son with him today. Encouragement does contribute to the bottom-line.

What makes this even more personal for me is my son, Jason, was also 23 at this same time. In addition, when I heard the news, Jason was 4000 miles away and had been for the previous four months. I thank God he has a mother, two sisters, father, and grandparents who are regular in their encouragement and communication. I hope his business leader is also a person that encourages him and is not so concerned about the daily tasks at hand that he forgets there is a young man behind the employee number—a young man that on any occasion can feel "hard pressed on every side, perplexed, persecuted and struck down."

Several mutual acquaintances indicated they called their son or daughter immediately after hearing of our friend's tragedy. I hope it was not the first call in a long time.

We should look in the mirror and evaluate ourselves as to the amount of encouragement we provide. Then we should increase it tenfold, as long as it is called "Today."

CHAPTER TEN

PERFECT LEADER QUALITY #10:
ALWAYS LEAVE A GIFT

"A gift opens the way for the giver and ush-
ers him into the presence of the great."

Proverbs 18:16

The Perfect Leader sets a very clear precedent when interfacing with individuals and groups. He always left them better off after meeting with Him than they were before the meeting. He provided to each a "gift." To some it was a word of kindness, to others it was a word of encouragement, to others knowledge, to others answers, to others food, to others rest, to others relief from illness, to others friendship, and to others eternal hope.

Without exception, people were richer for their encounter with The Perfect Leader. He soon was recognized as a giver and not a taker. His ability to read the needs and desires of his followers and to supply part or all of those solutions ushered Him into their presence, no matter what the time or place. They wanted to be around Him.

The Perfect Leader had a trust level that continued to grow daily. This was because his behavior demonstrated his underlying intent. With a leader so intent on meeting needs and leaving a person in an improved state, it is no wonder that his followers grew in numbers daily.

The key to being a great giver is to understand what the person needs and the value he places on that need. The individual frequently does not understand his own real need. For example, we ask our children to buckle up their seat belts when they get into the car. We recognize the potential dangers associated with auto accidents and the consequences to the passengers involved if they are not strapped in. Our children comply with this request, not because they feel a need to be safe, but because they trust our judgment. We know they have this need to be safe, therefore, we provide them this potential gift.

The Perfect Leader studied his followers to know their needs. He talked to them. He listened; He observed. He questioned, and as a result, He often understood their needs and problems better than they did.

> Matthew 6:8 "Do not be like them, for your Father knows what you need before you ask him."

What would it be like to have a leader who knows us well enough to know our needs in advance of our request?

THE PERFECT LEADER OR THE LONE RANGER

At first glance, we could think the Lone Ranger was a leader who always left a gift. After all, didn't he always leave a silver bullet behind after he completed his assignment? The problem is simple. How many of us want or need a silver bullet?

The Lone Ranger's silver bullet gift is a very good metaphor to describe what is wrong with many people in charge today. They have good intentions, but *their* gifts create dependency, not empowerment.

To get a silver bullet, several things had to happen. First, there had to be a significant problem. Second, I could not handle the problem myself. Third, the situation required rescue from an outsider. The rescuer preferred to fix my problem for me versus involving me in the process of learning to solve my problem. Fourth, the situation must appear hopeless. I had given up, obviously lacking the needed effort and skill, and yet the Lone Ranger saved the day, after the commercial break. Sixth, he left that stupid silver bullet for me to put on my mantle and remind me how useless, hopeless, and miserable I was until he came to my rescue!

So what did I learn? I learned that when I have a problem, call the Lone Ranger because I can't do it myself.

As a consultant, our firm puts a strong emphasis on teaching people to fish versus catching the fish for them. In a world of abundance, we will have other opportunities with these clients if we help them learn to handle the old problems. In addition, this is more of a partnership mentality and less of a vendor/buyer relationship. Our gift to our clients is often *equipping them* to do what they thought they needed us to do and *teaching them* to do it in our initial assignment. This elevates our value to them, and we are most often given the opportunity to work on even more critical and challenging issues.

Businesses that continually operate out of crisis and are dependent on a few "troubleshooters" to save the day are generally run by people who suffer from the silver bullet virus. The organization has little commitment to develop and train its people and even less real intent to fix problems on a permanent basis. After all, it may replace the boss who appears irreplaceable due to his fix-it-quick reputation. As Anton Chekhov once stated, "Any idiot can face a crisis; it is the day-to-day living that wears you out." No one else knows how or is capable of fixing the problem. This is called dependency, not leadership. The people frequently feel over managed and under led.

A crisis-oriented environment is the sustenance that fuels urgency addiction—an addictive high many crave.

When Jack Welch retired as the chief executive at General Electric, there was likely not a more respected business leader in the United States. By all measures, he would rate with the great names in American Industry management.

However, I would like to suggest that the greatness of Jack Welch and his true legacy is not only his performance, but also the performance of his successor, who was his follower. For then, his true leadership will be evident to all. How they deliver and continue to grow the vision will be the real test. Was Jack a charismatic, strong-willed manager or a visionary leader? There is no question as to his greatness as a CEO. While he was present to shape the activity at GE, his leadership stood out as one of the century's best. Since this is a book on leadership and not just management, we must watch the next generation before we can fully evaluate his leadership. For history to record him as a truly great leader (and not just a great manager), his impact must stretch to at least one more generation of GE leaders. The Perfect Leader model bridges generations and extends impact from Jesus to Billy Graham; now *that* is a legacy.

We have explored why the silver bullet was a failure as a gift. It was what the *leader* wanted to leave, not what the *receiver* wanted or needed. To be fair, we should examine what makes the gift of The Perfect Leader different and how we learn to provide this type of gift in our leadership arena.

The key to a gift of value is twofold. First, what is our motive for providing the gift? Finally, what is our focus?

The Perfect Leader establishes that the motive should be one of service (as was discussed in an earlier chapter) and a truly win-win approach. Many Scriptures discuss the phenomenon of giving.

> Luke 6:38 "Give, and it will be given to you. A good measure, pressed down, shaken together and running over, will be poured into your lap. For with the measure you use, it will be measured to you."

> Malachi 3:10 "Bring the whole tithe into the storehouse, that there may be food in my house. Test me in this," says the Lord Almighty," and see if I will not throw open the floodgates of heaven and pour out so much blessing that you will not have room enough for it."

There is no loser in the game of giving if the motive or intent is honorable and win-win.

It is obvious that we, as leaders, will benefit much from the idea of leaving a gift. However, if personal benefit is the true motive, it becomes a manipulative technique for self-gain. It is not the desire to see someone else prosper, feel better, or sense they are "richer" for the interaction. The Perfect Leader even gives us some warnings to watch our motives.

> James 4:2–3 "... You do not have, because you do not ask God. When you ask, you do not receive, because you ask with wrong motives, that you may spend what you get on your pleasures."

All of us have been around a true giver. This person is genuinely interested in us and takes it upon himself to make our lives "richer" through something he possesses or knows and is willing to share. Isn't this person fun to be around? If you have an opportunity to spend time with this person, it is a no-brainer. We make the time. He never makes you feel like you are interrupting his day or keeping him from pursuing some important task. In fact, you feel that *you* are that important task.

The Perfect Leader demonstrates this with every person He encounters. His empathy, concern, ability to listen, attentiveness, compassion, and willingness to share his ideals became the magnetic force that drew people of all careers and interests to become his followers. They were richer for the interaction.

So much for the motive; now what should the focus be?

As was discussed in chapter four, The Perfect Leader had a purpose and believed He was to continually advance the mission He was commissioned to fulfill. Therefore, every gift was, in one way or another, a link, promotion, or connection to his purpose or mission. If people were to see Him in light of his purpose, they must be able to link the gift He gave them either directly or indirectly with his mission.

It is easier to use our business to demonstrate the linkage

between the gift and the mission. For years, I have suggested to our salespeople, consultants, and trainers to leave a gift with the customer or prospect with whom they are interacting at the time.

Our mission is to help people and organizations understand and respond to change in a manner that ensures their (combined) future survival, individual performance, and fulfillment. Our products include consulting and training services in the leadership, management, sales, organizational development disciplines, and executive or managerial coaching arena. All of these lead to creating change strategies to fulfill our mission.

So what gifts could our staff leave with the customer or prospect? It should be a free gift that the receiver will feel is of value. It should make the customer feel richer, wiser, and better equipped because of his interaction with a De La Porte & Associates, Inc. employee.

The gifts can come in many forms. They include such things as white papers on research and experiences, which provide the latest thinking, an article from a magazine to give him a relevant connection to one of his problems, a reference that he can call to get a free opinion to help solve a common problem, a word of encouragement, a new piece of research that relates to his current challenges, a willing ear to listen, or an insight to his real problem when he had no idea that it existed. **To deliver this gift, the focus must be on the customer's need, not on what we are selling.**

The key is to understand what the customer really wants or needs. It is something that will make them feel richer for the time spent with the DLPA employee **AND** move them closer to our mission. This is a true win-win approach.

It should come as no surprise that the DLPA employees who model this behavior most consistently have little difficulty with scheduling follow-up meetings and fulfilling our mission. The customer knows the meeting will result in his enrichment. As The Perfect Leader told us, "A good measure pressed down, shaken together and running over . . ." We become an ally, not an inconvenience.

So with these current day examples, what are a few of the gifts that support the purpose of The Perfect Leader? A gift of healing, wine at the wedding feast, encouragement, a parable to bring a teaching to application, a revelation of the written law, a prayer for a friend, forgiveness of an enemy and finally, nothing less than his life. All of these are examples of gifts that heightened the awareness of his purpose to others. All these gifts were valued by the receiver, valued enough to make it into a book that has become the all-time best-seller, even 2000 years later.

What would our followers, employees, family, or friends say about our encounters with them? Would they feel "richer" for being with us, or would they describe us as a "taker"? Which actions and attitudes establish a person we would want to follow and call our leader?

IS IT REALLY MORE BLESSED TO GIVE
THAN RECEIVE?

It is more blessed to give than to receive. This is one of the most quoted sentences in our society concerning giving. The problem is clear. It seems we believe the opposite; our words, behaviors, and actions clearly demonstrate as an individual and as a society that we have a selfish nature.

It is likely we have legitimate excuses to model this selfish behavior and speak these self-serving words. After all, didn't we learn from infancy to cry out and demand our wishes? Later in life, we added such "skills" as pouting, comparing our situation to others, manipulation, controlling, and placing guilt on others to round out the "more blessed to receive" syndrome. We have created a group of people known as the "me generation"; if it feels good to me, then it must be okay to do it. We expect instant gratification, believing we can achieve and have anything that we set our minds to. Personal power and new age movements have redefined who "God" is to the many that practice these philosophies. We demand our rights, even if they impede others' rights. We criticize, blame, or attack when things don't go our way.

The bottom-line is that we are focused on getting not giving.

During many of the DLPA seminars in which we discuss leadership, we ask the participant to write down how he would like his epitaph to read. It is an activity that forces him to examine his actions and attitudes—the ones he currently demonstrates in his daily interactions. Once this is done, he can ask himself if his epitaph is likely to become a reality if he were to continue his current pattern of behavior. It is helpful to remind him that he will no longer be around to write it, so it must be done by someone else.

What amazes me is the frequency in which the person records statements such as, "I made a difference."

"I left the world a better place."

"I was a good parent and spouse."

The only way any of these statements can become a reality is by giving. The gift can take many shapes, but nonetheless, it is still a gift to a person, industry, society, or career field.

It appears we have a long-term desire to make a difference. This desire comes into direct conflict with our daily nature to be a receiver versus a giver.

Everyone has something to give. The Perfect Leader tells us that we all have a talent or skill, which we are to share and use for the betterment of those we meet.

> Romans 12:6–8 "We have different gifts, according to the grace given us. If a man's gift is prophesying, let him use it in proportion to his faith. If it is serving, let him serve; if it is teaching, let him teach; if it is encouraging, let him encourage; if it is contributing to the needs of others, let him give generously; if it is leadership, let him

govern diligently; if it is showing mercy, let him do it cheerfully."

It is obvious that we live in a world that creates many pressures and stressful schedules. It is very easy to be so focused on our problems and needs that we forget to take the time and make the choice to give our talents.

I learned a valuable lesson from my mother-in-law, Nettie Bass. By earthly standards, she was a woman who had very little. She had many opportunities to choose to focus on her own needs and problems. Yet she was so busy doing things for others, I don't think she knew how *poor* she was. During her funeral service, the family provided an open microphone for anyone who wished to say something about her life. It was incredible the number of people who stepped forward and expressed something she gave to each of them. Her gift was likely serving, and it was "all used up when she died." It was the longest and most joyful funeral I have ever attended. Her epitaph could have easily read, "Nettie Bass, she made a difference to everyone she met."

WHAT'S IN IT FOR ME?

It may appear from the Scriptures I have quoted that there is a tangible and financial guarantee to all this giving stuff. In other words, the giving serves as a sort of ante to get me into a bigger and more profitable game, insuring a significant gain. This is not the case. If the guarantee did exist, it would destroy any attempt to give with an unselfish motive. In reality, it would not be giving at all. It would be a form of personal investment and a return on the gift would be expected.

However, there is something in it, all you givers. There's a feeling deep within our being that we made a difference, created a smile, lightened the load, provided hope, etc. It's a feeling we could never duplicate without giving or investing a little of ourselves in another person.

Last night I picked up my voice mail. There was a message from my son, Jason. He was in Syracuse teaching a class, and I was in Orlando consulting with a client. His message made my year. "Dad, just calling to see how you are doing and thought we might rap for a while. I was thinking both Dawn and Kim (his sisters) have turned out great, and I was calling to get some advice on what you did so I can make sure I do some of those things with Kylar (his 8-month-old daughter); you know I don't know much about little girls."

What was that gift worth? You can't buy it; it's not for sale!

The Perfect Leader describes the benefits of being a giver. In the book of Proverbs, He clearly indicates the giver benefits most from the gift and prospers as a result of the act. It does not lay claim that this benefit takes the form of a tangible payback. In fact, it implies that the return on investment the giver receives is the change of internal feelings and attitude.

> Proverbs 11:24–25 "One man gives freely, yet gains even more; another withholds unduly, but comes to poverty. A generous man will prosper; he who refreshes others will himself be refreshed."

DISTRUST OF THE GIFT AND THE GIVER

A number of years ago I was making a sales call on a new prospect. I was ushered into his office and seated across the desk from him. He was very cordial, but I became distracted by the nicely framed poster that was behind him, over his right shoulder.

The poster showed a tough-looking cowboy with both his six-guns pulled and pointed directly at me. The caption below the poster read in bold letters, "We shoot every fifth salesman and the fourth just left." While I had a good laugh at the thought and creativity of the poster, it conveyed an all-to-subtle message. Someone believed that salespeople were in the business of taking, not giving.

This type of distrust of the gift and giver is often prevalent in organizations today. Most recently, one of our clients provided an unsolicited vacation benefit to his union employees. I participated in a few roundtable discussions with several of the senior management team and a few hundred of their hourly employees shortly after the announcement. During the discussion, the topic of this "gift" worked its way into the dialogue. The response from these workers was typical of what is communicated too frequently in the workplace today. "Sure, it was nice, but we don't believe you are doing this without a catch. When something else like this is done again, then we will start to believe it did not have strings attached."

It is this behavior and lack of appreciation that discourages many givers. If they are not seasoned givers, it is easy to change back to being takers, to give up, and to go back to status quo.

To be on the safe side, give with the expectation that no one will thank you, and you will not be disappointed with the lack of response. If you are expecting a thank you, then perhaps your motives should be checked.

The Perfect Leader experienced rejection, insult, indifference, and criticism from many of the people to which He gave gifts, but He still gave; in fact, He gave more.

THE INDESCRIBABLE GIFT

> II Corinthians 9:6–7 "Remember this: Whoever sows sparingly will also reap sparingly, and whoever sows generously will also reap generously. Each man should give what he has decided in his heart to give, not reluctantly or under compulsion, for God loves a cheerful giver."

So true giving comes from the heart and not from the mind.

A cheerful giver is a person who delights in the act of giving, a person who gives without knowing he is giving, and a person who gives as a way of life. This person will have no trouble finding followers.

Proverbs 18:16 "A gift opens the way for the giver
and ushers him into the presence of the great."

If you have the slightest doubt about this truth, think about
Mother Teresa, Reverend Billy Graham, or Gandhi. The foundation of their leadership was unselfish giving of themselves, their
time, and their talents. Yet they amassed millions of followers,
from peasants to kings.

As was our test for vision and mission, so is our test for giving. Did The Perfect Leader give? I think this book has already
validated the many ways that The Perfect Leader gave to his followers, friends, and acquaintances. However, there is still something even more special and unique about his gifts, namely, his
indescribable gift.

Fortunately, for each of us as leaders, we will not need to
give our lives to see our purposes, missions, and visions become
realities. Yet in the case of The Perfect Leader, that is exactly
what is recorded.

His purpose, as discussed in John 3:17, required Him to
come to this earth to save the world. Saving the world became
the giving of Himself in exchange for our sins.

The Perfect Leader made a choice and had the focus of clear
motives to provide a gift to all his followers—then, now, and
for all time. A cheerful giver, dedicated to sowing generously,
provided a gift that has ushered Him into every country, every
government, every language, every economic background (rich
or poor), and every social status (powerful or weak).

A sacrificial gift that only He could give, but all can
receive.

It is no wonder that for me and millions upon millions of
other followers, Jesus Christ is our leader—The Perfect Leader,
a model for today's leaders and tomorrow's leaders.

II Corinthians 9:15 "Thanks be to God for his
indescribable gift!"

The Perfect Leader!

GOOD LEADERS WERE FIRST GOOD FOLLOWERS

It is easier to be a great leader when you have great followers. In most cases, great leaders were first great followers. They learned from these experiences and then applied the lessons to their new roles as leaders. The following is a brief listing of characteristics modeled by effective followers. This list could be used to challenge your followers or to evaluate your own contribution as a follower. It may provide insights regarding your progression or lack of progression in becoming a leader. It might even be suggested that The Perfect Leader was also The Perfect Follower.

Characteristics of Great Followers

1. They listen and learn from their leader.
2. They are obedient.
3. They are patient for their opportunities, but they are ready when the opportunities present themselves.
4. They carry out their assignments with positive, can-do attitudes.
5. They give a full day's work for a full day's pay.
6. They represent their leader with commitment.
7. They perform—pursuing the vision, mission, and values, which they are charged to fulfill.
8. They demonstrate faith in their leader's leadership.
9. They are loyal.
10. They build their leader up through words and encouragement.

CHAPTER ELEVEN

THE LEADERSHIP
STAR MODEL

If each of us were to rate ourselves on a ten-point scale against the "10 characteristics" of The Perfect Leader, we would likely be discouraged and realize that perfection is not possible. It is time to remind ourselves that the call is to *aim for perfection*.

At the same time, it is fair to conclude there is only one Perfect Leader, and there will never be another perfect leader. So what should we do?

The following diagram takes the ten characteristics of The Perfect Leader and places them into an easy to understand model. Without taking the pencil off the paper, draw a five-point star like you did as a child. This figure will serve to represent the model for this twenty-first-century leader who wants to follow the example set by The Perfect Leader.

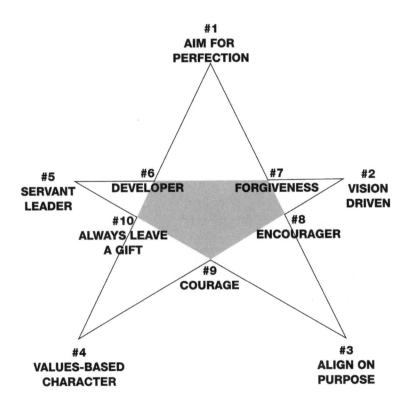

#1
AIM FOR
PERFECTION

#5
SERVANT
LEADER

#6
DEVELOPER

#7
FORGIVENESS

#2
VISION
DRIVEN

#10
ALWAYS LEAVE
A GIFT

#8
ENCOURAGER

#9
COURAGE

#4
VALUES-BASED
CHARACTER

#3
ALIGN ON
PURPOSE

Starting with the point at the top of the star and moving clockwise you will see five points. They represent the following:

(1)   Continual improvement by aiming for perfection
(2)   Creating the future by driving the vision
(3)   Always working on purpose or within the mission
(4)   The character of your business and personnel demonstrated as they model the values
(5)   The service attitude portrayed through all contact with other people and organizations

I will refer to these five points as "points of attack" (*points* because they have a penetrating characteristic, like an arrow, and *attack* because of the aggressive nature in which they influence both the spirit and attitude of a person). They represent the five characteristics that should be evident to all who might come in contact with you or your organization.

As we examine the model, it is time to examine the intersection points of the lines. The five intersection points are at the center of the model. It is no coincidence that they represent the core of the leader. The inside, shaded area of the model resembles a home plate in baseball. It is from this "home base" that the fortitude and focus is developed, which allows for the internal belief system of the leader to operate. Without this home base foundation, the points of attack are vulnerable.

This signifies an inside-out leader—one who first internalizes his beliefs and attitudes before he acts. His stance, decisions, and actions are an outcome of who he is and not from what or whom is trying to influence him.

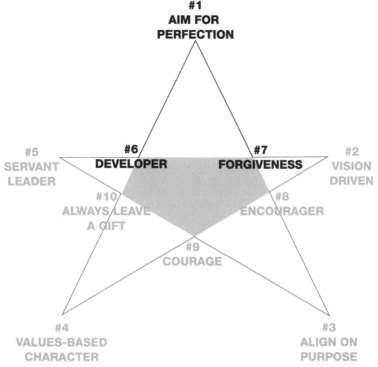

Starting at the 10:30 intersection, we discover the mindset of the leader as a developer. Moving to the 1:30 intersection, the forgiveness quality of the leader emerges. These two elements of our home base are necessary to support the point of attack, Aim for Perfection.

If we are going to ask our followers to strive for perfection and always (yes, always) improve, it is risky and tiring. They must never be satisfied with staying at a current level of performance, but they must improve daily. To do this, a leader must have at his core the commitment to invest in them, both with time and money. In addition, mistakes will be made, thus the leader must have an attitude of forgiveness. This will serve as the launch pad for the followers to strive continually for excellence.

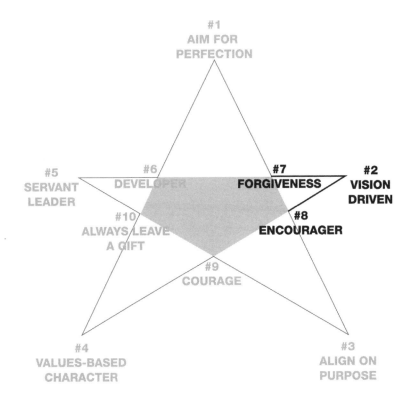

#1
AIM FOR
PERFECTION

#5
SERVANT
LEADER

#6
DEVELOPER

#7
FORGIVENESS

#2
VISION
DRIVEN

#10
ALWAYS LEAVE
A GIFT

#8
ENCOURAGER

#9
COURAGE

#4
VALUES-BASED
CHARACTER

#3
ALIGN ON
PURPOSE

Moving on to our 4:30 intersection, we will find the leadership quality of encouragement. This, added to the quality of forgiveness, supports the point of attack, vision. It is one thing to strive for excellence, but it is much scarier to commit to the unknown, step out in faith, and attempt to create the future—a future articulated through a vision for others to criticize, ridicule, and attempt to deny.

For a follower to believe in what he cannot see takes faith in the leader and his vision. Again, many setbacks, failures, and plans will go astray as the future is charted. The employee needs to know that his leader is a forgiver of mistakes, in pursuit of the future. In addition, the follower should see the leader as a constant encourager of his pursuits, endeavors, and mindset.

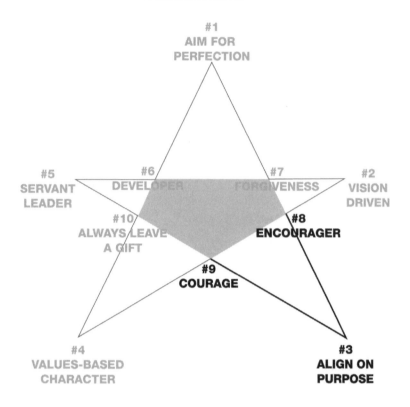

As we examine the intersection at 6:00, we find the element of courage. Courage along with encouragement is the home base element to support living and working on purpose. The follower must commit to always aligning his decisions and actions to the mission.

Encouragement is necessary to stay focused on the value-added activities within the mission. Courage is required to do the right thing, make the tough decision, and deny the desire to pursue non-value added activities, regardless of their attraction or pleasure. Without encouragement and courage, the follower will easily stray from the focused world of living on purpose and supporting the leader's mission.

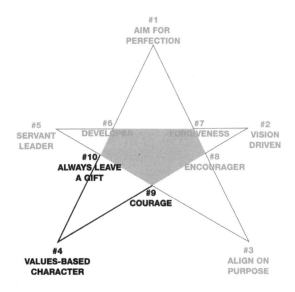

At the 7:30 intersection, we find the giver's attitude. As we connect this element to the quality of courage, we form the basis for our fourth point of attack, modeling a character that is value-based.

It is relatively easy to see how it takes courage to live one's values in all circumstances and in all situations, twenty-four hours a day. Nothing will encourage this behavior more strongly than knowing there is a gift waiting as a reward for this dedication—a gift that is intrinsic in most all circumstances. The gifts of thanks, appreciation, acceptance, or recognition are a few that reward a person at the most inward level of his being. The gift, on occasion, can also translate to something tangible: a raise, promotion, or added responsibility.

Let us not forget that in many situations, the greatest gift we give is to ourselves. It may be the feeling that we made a difference or that we contributed in an unexpected way or that a lesson was learned through our example. Whatever the gift, it gives us encouragement to continue the pursuit of a value-based character.

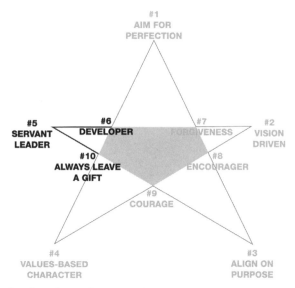

Our final point of attack is supported by the qualities of being a gift giver and being a developer. To be of service is a high calling and one that the receiver must believe to be genuinely offered.

The leader who can model the servant-leader style must be willing to invest in others, know others, and then serve others versus using them. Likewise, the leader who always gives more than he takes is easily seen as someone who is more attuned to serving another's needs versus being absorbed in his own pursuit of self.

The Leadership Star Model serves to remind us that The Perfect Leader's characteristics are qualities that today's leaders can develop with training and motivation. After all, Ephesians 5:1 tells us, "Be imitators of God . . ." In the language of this book, *be imitators of The Perfect Leader.*

With the thousands of leadership books that crowd the shelves of bookstores, I hope the qualities of The Perfect Leader will serve to empower your pursuit of leadership excellence. There may be more profound leadership books and more talented authors, yet without question—there is no better example than Jesus Christ, The Perfect Leader!

ADDITIONAL RESOURCES

If you would like more information on the topics reviewed in this book, please contact:

De La Porte and Associates, Inc.
1205 South White Chapel Blvd
Suite 200
Southlake, Texas 76092
817–481–9903

12015 Mountain Rd NE
Albuquerque, NM 87112
505-298-1787

www.delaporte.com

Also available through Allagi Learning, Inc.:

The Perfect Leader Workshop

The Perfect Leader 360 degree leadership assessment

Church workshops are available in 4- & 8-hour versions.

APPENDIX

The Values of De La Porte and Associates, Inc.

Model Christian Ethics
Be willing to serve others
Provide honest and loving communication
Treat people with dignity and respect
Assume good intentions
Forgive–unless you're perfect

Encourage Teammates Daily
Be a team player
Deliver two positives for every negative
Be each other's advocates
Be positive with mental resolve
Be sincere

Balance Personal Priorities
Work hard, play hard
Protect your health
Protect your spiritual well-being
Protect your family relationships
Grow your mental capabilities

Err on the Side of Action
Act within our Vision, Mission, Values
Over-communicate
Make decisions for greater good
Always play win/win/win
Keep your promises

Exceed Customer Expectations
Give more than you receive
Deliver on the contract
Service internal and external customers
Always leave a gift
Help them grow

Walk the Talk
Learn our technology
Model our teachings
Live our values
Know there are consequences for every action
Develop others to know your skills

Resolve Pinches Quickly
Clarify expectations
Be easy on the people
Be hard on the problem
Nip it in the bud
Avoid being a nit picker
Do the right thing
Treat the business as your own
Value all people
Work within our Vision, Mission, Values
Be 100% aligned with DLPA
Be willing to challenge the status quo
Create the Future
Reputation counts long-term
Be willing to stretch
Demonstrate a learning attitude
Apply and grow your skills
Challenge our system, respectfully
High Performance is the only Option
Meet your commitments
Contribute to our sales effort
Secure our customers through delivery
Be the best in your role
Be a high-activity self-starter

ENDNOTES

[1] From the January 29, 1996, issue of *Newsweek,* page 47. "A Quick Rx for Apple" by Steven Levy.

[2] Barker, Joel Arthur. The Power of Vision: Discovering the Future. Burnsville: ChartHouse International Learning Corporation. 1991

[3] Bennis, Warren G., and Burt Nanus. Leaders: the strategies of taking charge. New York: Harper & Row, Publishers, Inc.

[4] Ziglar, Zig. *See You at The Top.* Gretna: Pelican Publishing Company, 2003.

Contact De La Porte and Associates
or order more copies of this book at

TATE PUBLISHING, LLC

127 East Trade Center Terrace
Mustang, Oklahoma 73064

(888) 361 - 9473

Tate Publishing, LLC

www.tatepublishing.com